LEABHARLANNA CHONTAE FHINE GALL
FINGAL COUNTY LIBRARIES

Items should be returned on or before the last date shown below. Items may be renewed by personal application, by writing or by telephone. To renew give the date due and the number on the barcode label. Fines are charged on overdue items and will include postage incurred in recovery. Damage to, or loss of items will be charged to the borrower.

Date Due	Date Due	Date Due
08. DEC 95	*Office*	
01. FEB 96		
20. MAR		
12. NOV 97		
10. JAN 98	31.	
02. JUN 99		
18. OCT 00	24. FEB 06	
To FW return → ME. 18. 05. 01		

Edmund Rice

The Man and His Times

Desmond Rushe

Gill & Macmillan

Gill & Macmillan
Goldenbridge
Dublin 8
with associated companies throughout the world
First published 1981
Reprinted 1981
Second edition 1995
© Desmond Rushe 1981, 1995
0 7171 2372 3 (oo ᒐ
Cover design by Bill Bolger
Print origination by Typeform Ltd, Dublin
Printed by ColourBooks Ltd, Dublin

A catalogue record is available for this book from the British Library.

Contents

Preface

It is an honor, surely, to be invited to preface a biography of Edmund Ignatius Rice. We who are alumni of the Irish Christian Brothers schools and equally of those conducted by the Presentation Brothers are, in a sense, his living biography. Each of us reflects some facet of his hopes. He might well say with Paul in his second letter to the Corinthians (3:2) – 'You are my letter, known and read by all men, written on your hearts.'

The telling of his story is timely. Though it has been long delayed, it is very pertinent to our day and time. There is a new dimension to the position of the layman in the Church. The focus on family life in pastoral theology is a healing for an open wound in our society. The education of the young and of the poor is of perennial concern. The component of suffering, failure and rejection is a necessary sharing of the way, the truth and the life that leads to holiness.

As always, these elements must be incarnated in the lives of individuals. From among his children, our Heavenly Father selects certain ones who will exemplify these factors in a life span. In the United States, Elizabeth Ann Seton was such a one. She was socialite, wife, mother, widowed, impoverished, disowned, converted, and through it all, led by God to the founding of a Religious Community for the education of young and poor girls. She died in 1821 at the age of 47. Edmund Rice was a counterpart and contemporary. He was a man of wealth, social prestige, married, a father, a widower, an educator and a servant of the cross. The year that saw Mother Seton die was the year that Ignatius became the founder and General of the Society which he founded. His concerns surfaced through the troubled times at the turn of the century and beyond, but climaxed in the culture of our own times.

The Vatican Council Decree on the Renewal of Religious Life (No. 2) states: 'The spirit and aims of each founder should be faithfully accepted and retained, as indeed should each institute's sound traditions, for all these constitute the patrimony of an institute.' It is to record and preserve this patrimony that these pages are now produced. Inheritors of the spirit of Ignatius Rice in every continent will rejoice at this event.

The holiness of this man will appear through these pages. May they stimulate us to pray that the heroic extent of his sanctity will find recognition in the Church and that in God's good time, we may venerate him in sainthood.

Timothy Cardinal Manning
Archbishop of Los Angeles
29 December 1980

Introduction

When I wrote the Introduction to the first edition of this book
in 1981, I referred to Edmund Rice. I can now hope to refer
to Blessed Edmund, because the cause for his canonisation
has progressed almost to the stage of beatification. And if I
live to a ripe old age and yet another edition is called for,
perhaps I may refer to him as Saint Edmund. But, for the
moment, it is Edmund; and it is startling to remember that
he was a hugely successful businessman and entrepreneur in
his day and that, by today's money values, he would certainly
have been, or have had the potential to become, a millionaire.
It is not often that wealth and sanctity find a close human
association: they did so uniquely in the case of Edmund.

It is as difficult to visualise a modern equivalent of Edmund
Rice as it is to relate modern living conditions to those which
governed the mass of the people around the turn of the 19th
century. But if the times then were extraordinary in terms of
human misery, the man was even more extraordinary in terms
of transcendent quality. He is paralleled, not by any
contemporary figure one can think of, but, in an inverted type
of way, by a person in the New Testament.

The story of the rich young man has been described by
Wilfred Harrington, O.P., as the saddest and one of the most
human in the Gospel of St Mark. It is the well known story of
the good-living young man who aspired to become a disciple
of Christ and was told that, if he would be perfect, he should
'go, sell what you have and give to the poor . . . and come,
follow me'. The young man's face fell when he heard this and
he went away sorrowful, for he had great possessions. A sad
story indeed, and a very human one.

The inverted parallel arises because what the rich young man found impossible to do was done in a precise and literal way by Edmund Rice. He *did* sell what he had; he *did* give to the poor and he *did* follow Christ. And he followed Christ in a manner which, in keeping with his remarkable talent for mixing the idealistic and the feasible, was spiritually productive and materially practical to equally high degrees. He sold his up-market house and his thriving and expanding business, and devoted the proceeds to the welfare of the most wretched of God's children. He devoted himself as well, exchanging the comforts of his home for a bleak room in a stable loft. In a totally meaningful way, he became the rich young man accepting Christ's austere invitation and the total self-renunciation that went with it.

When I was asked by the Irish Christian Brothers to write a life of their Founder, I knew scarcely anything about the man. I had not attended a Christian Brothers' school and the name of Edmund Rice meant little. But, by degrees, I came to know him as one of the great figures in Irish history. In his admirably practical way, he identified education as the *sine qua non* to the realisation of human dignity, the fulfilment of human destiny and the attainment of human freedom, and in his admirably visionary way, he committed himself to doing something about it. Against impossible odds, political, financial and technical, he initiated an educational system which profoundly influenced Ireland and helped change the course of its history, and which became worldwide in its ramifications.

There was a difficulty in coming to grips with the subject himself on an intimate, human level because of an almost total lack of personal material relating to his inner thoughts and emotions. He was an extremely reticent person but he was, clearly, a person of quiet but dazzling charisma. How else could he have attracted others to join him in his absurd scheme to educate wretchedly poor and wild young illiterates? How else could he have inspired generations of Brothers to deny themselves, as they are still joyously doing today, and to join with him in following Christ through an apostolate to the poor and deprived?

What follows is an attempt to chronicle the works of Edmund Rice, and to place it into the perspective of its time. While every effort has been made to maintain the highest level of factual accuracy and a reasonable degree of objectivity, it does not pretend to be the definitive biography: for instance, it only skirts around the edges of Edmund Rice's immense spirituality. It could not have been written without the help so warmly given by many Christian Brothers and, particularly, without the vast amount of material collected by the gentle Brother M. C. Normoyle over years of exhaustive research and made available with great generosity.

Desmond Rushe
March 1995

A Land of Suffering

Because of religious, political and social repression, the conditions under which the great majority of the Irish in Ireland existed during the eighteenth century were cruelly grim. But there were some small oases of prosperity and comfort in the bleak and general desert of poverty and misery, and one such oasis could be found in the townland of Westcourt near Callan in Co. Kilkenny. Here the Rice family lived; they were industrious and respected people, and they worked a considerable area of good land to a high degree of efficiency and success. Their home was, in relative terms, quite out of the ordinary in proportions, amenities and comforts: built around 1676, it was a long, low, thatched house with hipped gables and massively solid walls made from yellow clay mixed with horsehair and straw for greater durability. There were four bedrooms, a spacious parlour, a large kitchen with a splendid open hearth, and a hallway. The external facilities were in keeping with the levels of indoor well-being – cow shed, stable, hen-house, hay barn, dairy, kitchen garden and orchard, paddock and, set in a cobble-stone yard, a well which provided a plentiful supply of pure water for drinking and domestic purposes.

It can be assumed that the house was equipped and furnished in a manner fitting to the status of a family which enjoyed a living standard that was, at the very least, reasonably high. And as the Rices involved themselves in their husbandry with a quiet and hard-working application, it can also be assumed that they were never short of wholesome and varied food. They minded their own business, and they minded it well; they liked good land, and they worked it well. The range of their farming activities included the growing of wheat, oats, potatoes and flax; the raising of cattle, sheep, pigs and poultry. Wheat was ground and made into bread; milk was churned and the cream made into butter; cloth was spun and hens laid eggs. In dramatic contrast to hordes of their fellow Catholics, the Rices were self-sufficient, well housed and well fed.

Edmund Rice was born in the bedroom to the left of the cottage's entrance hallway in June 1762, the fourth of seven sons, and a few days later was taken to be baptised in the modest Stone House by the Green, as the parish church of Callan was known. It was a two-storey building which gave no outward indication that it was a place of worship. The floor was of trampled yellow clay, and its furnishings were limited to a plain wooden altar. There was no kneeling or seating accommodation, and the Parish Priest, Fr James Butler, lived in an austere room overhead whenever he considered it prudent to live there at all. The mean state of the church and the frequent absences of the priest were symptomatic of the manner in which Catholics and their religion were treated by official ordinance, and it was also symptomatic that when Robert Rice took his newly-born son to be baptised, he had to pay 'sacrament money' to the local Protestant rector. The end of the Penal Days had not yet come.

The Rices were an esteemed Kilkenny family. The name first appeared in official records when, in 1665–6, the Hearth Tax Rolls for the townland of Sunhill near Cuffesgrange listed three Rices and one Rhys, but it is more than likely that the line had a much longer history. Subsequently, the name became established in other areas, and by 1820 thirteen families of Rices farmed roughly 1,000 acres of land between Callan and Gowran – good land capable of yielding excellent fruits when industriously used. That the Rices applied themselves industriously is not in doubt, and equally there is no doubt that they were highly regarded, for at a time when even the most insignificant of offices were denied to Catholics, a number of them received appointments of a minor public nature.

Patrick Rice, Edmund's granduncle, farmed nearly one hundred acres at Attatinoe near Callan, partly acquired from Lord Desart and partly by deed of the Protestant Dean of

Callan, the Reverend Thomas Chandler. His brother Edmund settled at Westcourt with his family of three sons and one daughter, and his standing was given a measure of recognition when he was appointed a toll official for the town and liberties of Callan in 1754. His property passed in 1757 to Robert Rice, Edmund's father, who then had a substantial tract of land leased from Lord Desart, and Robert was also evidently well thought of, because he became a market juror of Callan.

The Tierneys were another old and respected Catholic family. They too had settled at Westcourt, and when one of the daughters, Margaret, married a Mr Murphy, the couple took up residence in the Tierney Westcourt home. Two daughters were born of the marriage, but following the early death of Mr Murphy, Margaret later married Robert Rice. Two well known families were united as a result, and their combined properties became one. The area involved was roughly 160 acres, for which Robert Rice paid an annual rent of £300, but the most important, far-reaching and enduring outcome of the marriage was the birth of Edmund Rice. In later years of dedication, unwavering perseverance, suffering and travail, he was to exercise an astonishing influence in educational and religious areas in Ireland and many parts of the world. The story of Edmund Rice's spiritual growth and practical achievement is one of immense significance, and it is all the more remarkable when set against his comfortable childhood and his attainments as an eminently successful businessman.

He was born in a period of appalling deprivation and degradation. Since the final collapse of the old Gaelic order, the history of Ireland had been one of almost totally unrelenting sorrow and while there were phases of comparative ease, a general pattern of savage suppression and exploitation became established. The Puritan Government of 1641 had decreed the absolute suppression of the Catholic religion in Ireland, and the rebellion of the same year had been crushed with devastating savagery. Cromwellian massacres were carried out for the greater glory of God, and the best land was confiscated for division between new Protestant settlers and unscrupulous adventurers. Even after the Ulster plantation in

Ireland: important towns and places associated with Edmund Rice

the time of James I, two-thirds of cultivable land remained in the hands of Catholics, but after Cromwell, three-quarters passed to a small minority of Protestants.

The restoration of the monarchy in 1660 raised hopes, but while Catholics enjoyed for a time a more tolerant religious atmosphere, the law relating to land ownership stayed as it was. Under James II in the 1680s there was a renewal of hope. A Catholic Viceroy was appointed, Catholics were admitted to important administrative offices, and an Irish parliament dominated by Catholics passed an act reversing the Cromwellian land settlement. It was a piece of legislation which gave favoured Protestants a fright, but it never came into force. The successes of William of Orange at Aughrim and the Boyne brought disastrous consequences for Catholics, and after the Treaty of Limerick in 1691 a further round of confiscations placed more land in the hands of Protestants. It is on record that in 1688 the Catholic majority owned only 22 per cent of their country's land, but by 1703 the share had dwindled to around 15 per cent. By the middle of the eighteenth century it had shrunk to 7 per cent, and in 1778 it stood at 5 per cent.

The theft of land was only a part of the overall scandal. The Puritan government had decreed the total suppression of the Catholic religion in Ireland, and an inevitable effect was that those who chose to remain Catholic would be deprived of many basic human rights. According to the Protestant historian W. E. H. Lecky, the object of the Penal Code was 'to make the Catholic majority poor and to keep them poor . . . to degrade them into a servile state'. A particularly vicious equivalent of apartheid was put in place centuries before another form of apartheid was universally condemned, and Protestant domination of Catholic Ireland was nearly absolute.

Catholics were excluded from all public life and from much normal social activity. Any form of Catholic education was forbidden, and it was illegal for a Catholic to buy land, obtain a mortgage on it, rent it at a reasonable profit or inherit it in the accepted manner. When a Catholic landowner died, his estate could not pass to his eldest son but had to be divided equally among all his sons, and if any of the sons became Protestant, he automatically inherited the entire estate. A wife who turned Protestant could claim part of her husband's holding, and should a Catholic make a profit in excess of one-third of his rent, he could lose his lease to the first Protestant who would inform against him. A Catholic was not permitted to rent land on a lease of more than thirty-one years. Not only did the Penal Laws prevent Catholics from acquiring land by purchase, but they also contained provisions which made the continued leasing of land a matter of considerable difficulty, especially when the land was competently and profitably used.

The deliberate debasement of Catholics could be seen in many other areas as well. They could not join the army or navy; they could not vote or be elected to parliament; they could not enjoy any office of State. Those of them who had been able to lead the lives of country gentlemen found themselves subject to the penalty of whipping should a sporting gun be found in their possession, and they could not keep a horse worth more than £5. Priests were banished from the country and should they return and be discovered, they were liable to be hanged, drawn and quartered. Bounties were offered for the capture of clergy and a priest-hunting traffic was actively encouraged. Mass could be celebrated only in isolated bogs or on lonely mountain sides, and almost the only education available to Catholic children was provided by wandering teachers who set up hedge schools.

In a campaign unparalleled for its inhumanity, Catholics were reduced to an animal status, and the Chief Baron of the Exchequer, John Bowes, could say with perfect truth in 1759 that the law did not presume an Irish Catholic to exist, 'except for the purpose of punishment'. The same woeful policy applied on the economic level. In 1699 the export of woollen goods – a primary manufacture – was forbidden except to England, and prohibitive import duties were imposed there. The Irish peasant was reduced to abject slavery. He had no rights; he was subjected to extortionate rents; he had no redress against arbitrary eviction and, should his talents and industry lead to improved living standards, he faced ever-higher rents or dispossession.

So poverty, squalor and demoralisation grew. In 1720 Dean Swift described the condition of the Irish tenant as being worse than that of the English beggar: 'The landlords by unmeasurable screwing and racking their rents all over the kingdom have already reduced the poor people to a worse condition than the peasants of France or the vassals of Germany or Poland. . . . Whoever travels this country and observes the face of nature, or the faces and habits and dwellings of the natives, will hardly think himself in a land where law, religion or common humanity is professed.' Near the same time, the Protestant Bishop of Derry recorded: 'Never did I behold, even in Picardy, Westphalia or Scotland, such dismal marks of hunger and want as appeared in the countenances of the poor creatures I met on the road.' In similar vein, the Protestant Bishop and philosopher, George Berkeley asked in *The Querist* whether there could be 'on the face of earth any Christian or civilised people so beggarly, wretched and destitute as the common Irish'.

Edmund Rice was only two years old when a Dublin gentleman, J. Bush, wrote of the exploitation of the peasantry by the middleman, and commented: 'The condition of the lower class of farmer is little better than a state of slavery.' Six years later the then Viceroy stated: 'I had hoped to be excused from representing to His Majesty the miserable situation of the lower ranks of his subjects in this Kingdom. What from the rapaciousness of their unfeeling landlords and the restrictions on their trade, they are amongst the most wretched people on earth.' Then in 1787 the Protestant Attorney General, FitzGibbon, described the poor of Munster as 'being in a state of oppression, abject poverty, sloth, dirt and misery not to be equalled in any part of the world'.

The state of Ireland was clearly at a horrifically low ebb. There was little evidence that here was a proud, valiant and talented race of people, or that here was a country once known as the Island of Saints and Scholars, whose missionaries brought light to Europe in its dark age or whose artists and craftsmen left the world a legacy of dazzling beauty. A French visitor, Chevalier De La Tocnaye, came in the 1790s and was shocked by the nakedness of the poor and by the hovels in which they lived, which did not seem made for human beings at all. They might well have been hard-working and industrious, he wrote, had there been any hope of work improving their lot, but he remarked that if they produced more, the landlord put up their rent. He added: 'When reduced to starvation, is it not better to do nothing if the most assiduous labour can do nothing to prevent it?' He noted with understanding that the excessive drinking to which the peasantry were given was simply a form of Lethe and their apathy no more than the habit of despair.

Callan, in the valley of the King River, was a considerable town. A region of good tillage and dairy land, the countryside around was noted for its quiet, natural beauty. An outpost of the Pale, it had been a walled town, loyal to the crown and to its Ormond overlords. It had been given a charter in 1217 when it was incorporated by Earl William Marshall, and it had a 'Corporation of Sovereign, Burgesses and Freemen'. It had two bailiffs and a town clerk, was self-administered and was entitled to hold fairs, levy tolls and enjoy the privileges of the feudal system. It had turnpikes which were under the control of the local landlords, and in earlier times it had been the scene of battles between the kings of Ossory and Munster. Later, an Irish town had come into existence outside its walls on the northern side.

A Captain Geoghegan and fifteen hundred followers perished in defending it against Cromwellian forces, and it experienced the horrors which marked the progress of Cromwell's butchering men. On the restoration of Charles II, the Duke of Ormond recovered the estates he had lost through the influence of a nephew, Colonel John Butler, but by the end of the eighteenth century, the decline of Callan as an important centre was under way. The walls had disappeared and in a population of roughly two thousand adults as many as one thousand were unemployed. The town had small industries – a flour mill, an iron foundry, a small distillery and two tanneries – but because of early marriages and large families, the employment available was very much inadequate to the needs of the labour market.

The local populace depended mainly for work on nearby landlords, of whom there were approximately seventy in Co. Kilkenny and ten in the Callan area. The annual wage in the latter part of the eighteenth century was about £5 a year for men and £2.50 for women, and when seasonal work was available, the earnings were a few pence a day. In times of persistently recurring hardship, migrants came to offer themselves for hire, and these spalpeens, as they were known, were by no means welcomed by unemployed townspeople. Violent clashes were not uncommon, and Callan earned itself a reputation which was probably not fully justified. 'Callan of the ructions' it was called, and there was a saying: 'Walk through Ireland, but run through Callan.' It is likely that, given the conditions that obtained generally throughout the country, the same sort of strife was widespread, and it is probable that, as harsh as the position was in Callan, it was even worse elsewhere.

There is, however, no doubt that Callan had its share of hardship and suffering. In his *Statistical Observances Relative to the County of Kilkenny*, William Tighe painted a vividly grim picture. He described the town with its two main streets, connecting laneways and the hovels in which the majority of the people lived their desolate lives: 'Like too many of the peasants in the south of Ireland, they are miserably lodged; there are numbers of them who have not a bedstead, not even what is called a truckle-bed frame; a pallet to sleep on is a comfort unknown to them; a wad of straw or perhaps heath laid on a damp floor forms their resting place; but very few of them have anything like sheets; their blankets are generally wretchedly bad; in short the bed cloths are ragged and scanty; they put their coats and petticoats over them in aid of their blankets in cold weather, too often they are still damp having been but imperfectly dried by a miserable fire after they were worn at work in the rain.'

That scene bears no relationship at all to the life of the Rices a short distance out the road. In their home, as in the homes of all the better-class country community, there were warm beds, bright fires, good and wholesome food, home-grown fruit and farm produce, the opportunity for children to play and to experience the security and glow of the close family circle. The Rices were inevitably aware of the awful circumstances of their neighbours, circumstances which persisted for many years into the future. Edmund Rice was seventy-two when H. D. Inglis wrote of Callan in 1834: 'I have not yet seen in Ireland any town in so wretched a condition as this. I saw the people crawling out of their hovels – they and their hovels not one shade better than I have seen in the sierras of Granada where the people live in holes excavated in the banks. Their cabins were mere holes with nothing within them except a little straw and one or two broken stools – ranges of hovels without a ray of comfort or a trace of civilization about them, and people either in a state of actual starvation or barely keeping body and soul together.'

Before the end of the eighteenth century, the Kilkenny-born Amhlaoibh O Suilleabhain – poet, diarist and wandering schoolteacher – arrived in Callan and began to teach in a crude cabin which neighbours built in three days: the sod walls on the first, rafters and roof timbers on the second and the roof on the third. He recorded that in the currency of the time, 'a miserable stone of potatoes' cost 5½d, a barrel of oats 18/– and the poor people were without work or pay to buy any kind of food. 'There are not even alms for the paupers', he wrote. 'They are being sent off home, to their own parishes. Callan's own paupers, who number three hundred families or fifteen hundred persons, are reduced to misery. . . . I hope to God people's hearts will soften. Three hundred families in Callan are starving. . . . A poor, hungry crowd tried to take meal from the boats which were sailing from Clonmel to Carrick-on-Suir, but the peelers fired on them from the boats. Three of the poor Irishmen were killed and six others very badly wounded.' He added with striking poignancy: 'The Irishman's spirit is greatly broken. Hunger.'

The spirit was not quite broken. There were some rising up to revive and foster it. Edmund Rice was one. He would turn his back on the comparative luxury of Westcourt and devote himself, his formidible strength and his enormous talents to those who were even more wretched, if such were possible, than the unfortunate paupers of Callan.

2

The Early Years

The operation of the Penal Laws varied from time to time and from place to place, and there were districts in Ireland where they were applied with viciousness. There were landlords with magisterial powers who controlled vast areas of confiscated land and who, through greed, fear and a spurious notion of superiority were determined to hold what they had acquired or inherited, and to exploit it to the fullest possible extent. Backed by the power of the legislative machine, they adopted a policy of terror to ensure that their revenues and their power would in no way be diminished, and some of their names are still etched in the folk memory as synonyms of cruelty and infamy. But where the Protestant ascendancy was tolerant or humane, or at least indifferent, the laws were applied less ruthlessly, and in this respect Callan fared a great deal better than most areas.

An Augustinian monastery had been established in the town around 1468 and, according to record, was noted for its learned community and its library, rich in manuscripts, and possessing duplicates of all the rare books in the library of Jerpoint, the celebrated Cistercian foundation which dated from the twelfth century. It was also noted for 'the richness of its church utensils but, above all, for its care of the poor'. Following the suppression of the monasteries in 1540, the Augustinians maintained a connection with Callan, however tenuous, and on the Restoration, the monastery was re-established. The new foundation was of such importance that a General Chapter for the Augustinians of Ireland was held there in 1673.

So the friars remained, and while priests were few in Co. Kilkenny as a whole and Mass had frequently to be celebrated in the open, as in the Mass Quarry of Cooliath, Callan appears to have retained a favoured position. Following a relaxation of Penal Laws the *Abstract of the State of Popery* in 1766 recorded that there were three diocesan priests in Callan with four others serving the chapel of the Augustinian friars in Cloodeen Lane. The Augustinians had a close relationship with the Rices and one in particular often visited the Rice home at Westcourt. He was Father Patrick Grace, known as the Braithrin Liath – the little grey friar – because of his small stature and his premature greyness. He had been a dominie, or schoolmaster, before he took Holy Orders, and when he died at the age of ninety years, his reputation for holiness was widely known.

From the day of his birth, Edmund Rice's life was profoundly influenced by an unswerving family loyalty to the Catholic faith, and in this the Braithrin Liath undoubtedly played his part. The Tudor attempt to extend English Protestantism to Ireland was, as an historian has pointed out, a total failure, and when the lawyer and politician, Henry Flood, referred in the latter part of the eighteenth century to 'the Protestant nation of Ireland', he was referring to no more than a privileged and powerful minority. Some Catholics had embraced Protestantism to retain their hereditary property, and others had left the Catholic faith for more discreditable, mercenary reasons.

There were some in between who made the transition with a heavy heart and a troubled conscience, and this was clearly the case as regards the poet Piaras MacGearailt, who died in 1791. In his case, he succumbed to the inducements offered most unhappily, for he wrote: ''Tis sad for me to cleave to Calvin or perverse Luther, but the weeping of my children, the spoiling them of flocks and land, brought streaming floods from my eyes and descent of tears.' MacGearailt went on to talk of an aspect of converting which was plainly very painful to him and which, in a broader context, gives an insight into why the majority recoiled from deserting the old faith: 'There is a part of the Saxon Lutheran religion which, though not from choice, I have accepted that I do not like – that never a petition is addressed to Mary, the mother of Christ, nor honour, nor privilege, nor prayer, and yet it is my opinion that it is Mary who is (the) tree of lights and crystal of Christianity, the glow and precious lantern of the sky, the sunny chamber in the house of glory, flood of graces and Cliona's wave of mercy.' But the total number of those who changed allegiance was estimated at no more than 4,000. The vast majority of the old Gaelic stock persevered in an obstinate adherence to Catholicism, to the See of Peter, to devotion of the Mass and to Our Lady. *Semper fidelis* – always faithful – became established as a motto and when Pope John Paul II referred to it at the end of the first Papal visit to Ireland he was recalling in a special way the unshakable attachment shown by families like the Rices of Westcourt.

Like their forebears, they stood firm. After breaking the siege of Drogheda in 1649, Cromwell ordered all of its defenders – and women and children who could not be numbered among them – to be slaughtered, and he reported to Parliament: 'I am persuaded that this is a righteous judgement of God upon these barbarous wretches.' *Barbarous* was an adjective which had long been applied to the native Irish. They had been held in increasing contempt from Elizabethan times, and in 1575 John Derrick was being relatively mild when he confessed that 'My soul doth detest their wild shamrock manners.' The Penal Laws, designed to disarm, disinherit and discredit the Catholic population as a whole, and to exterminate the last remnants of the Catholic aristocracy, had done their best – or their worst – but despite them and their elements of dungeon, fire and sword (in writing about their injustice and inhumanity, Robert Kee noted in *The Green Flag* that one of their proposals related to the castration of priests), the attitude of *Semper fidelis* became more entrenched.

There was a gradual easing of the Penal Laws in the period before Edmund Rice's birth and youth, but there is an irritating lack of detail as to how his youth was spent. He was all through his life very reticent on a personal level, and he left remarkably little biographical information. The visits to Westcourt by the Braithrin Liath are known, and it is a reasonable assumption that they had a substantial bearing on the fact that Edmund's younger brother, John, became an Augustinian priest. Despite the scarcity of material, it is possible, however, to speculate with reasonable credibility what life in the Rice home was like, and what factors influenced Edmund in his early, sensitive and formative years. In this, oral tradition is a help.

The family was, as has been noted, very comfortable. They worked approximately 160 acres of good land diligently, and there was no shortage of food and clothing. They were, clearly, a united family and it is also clear that much attention was paid to an inculcation of spiritual values. The children played their games and adult conversation must frequently have been concerned with the state of the country and its recent history. The savagery of the Cromwellian conquest was fresh in the folk mind and only eighty years previously had St Oliver Plunket been hanged, drawn and quartered at Tyburn following a trial which showed an astonishing contempt for truth, justice and honour. Edmund Rice was just four years old when Father N. Sheehy, parish priest of Clogheen, Co. Tipperary, was charged with 'administering the oath of allegiance on behalf of the King of France and with the murder of one John Bridge'.

After undergoing torture, Fr Sheehy was hanged, drawn and quartered in Clonmel on 15 March 1766, and his head was placed on a spike outside the jail. That would have been talked about; so also would the case of local priest-hunters. A priest-hunter called Wise lived at Tullamaine, a mile from Westcourt, and another, Elliott, operated from Newtown, three miles away. Each had a detachment of soldiers under his command. They were in a lucrative business, for Dr Nicholas Madgett, Bishop of Kerry from 1753 to 1774 noted in a manuscript that survives that in his day, rewards offered included '£30 sterling or current money for a simple priest: £50 for a bishop: £40 for a vicar-general and £50 for a Jesuit'.

Other topics of conversation would have concerned recurrent tithe troubles. The Protestant rector in Callan had an annual income of £1,600 from tithes – a handsome sum at the time – and the Rices were obliged to pay their share twice yearly, in May and November: ten shillings per acre for potatoes, wheat and barley; six shillings per acre for meadow; three pence each for sheep and six pence each for lambs.

Another cause of unrest and discussion was the appropriation of common land by landlords who then proceeded to lease it at high rents, and yet another, the growing incidence of secret societies. They existed or were being formed under different names throughout almost the entire country, and when one such group announced that members would attend at all chapel gates in the diocese of Ossory to sign on recruits and administer the oath on Sunday, 27 August 1786, the bishop, Dr J. Troy, ordered that the chapels should remain closed and that no Mass should be celebrated. There was another talking point in 1764 when John Butler of Garryricken, who was well known in the Callan district, declared his intention to become a Protestant. On Sunday, 16 December, he set out for the Protestant church in Golden, riding in a splendid carriage drawn by four black geldings and attended by two men in full livery. He was ceremoniously received into the Protestant religion and, in the following year, was elected a member of parliament for Golden with the title of Earl of Ormond. In his case, the pay-off was particularly handsome.

Edmund Rice's earliest education came from his mother. The family attended Mass whenever possible in either the chapel by the Green or in the Augustinian friary, where priests preached 'alternately in Irish and English, but always in Irish if they were desirous to be understood'. It was probably to Callan that young Edmund also went for his modest initiation into formal education, though no record exists of his having done so. The school, in Moate Lane, measured 20 feet by 15 feet, and its doorway was its only lateral aperture, for whatever windows there were had been closed up. There were different scales of charges for pupils in schools of this type, e.g. $1/7\frac{1}{2}$ per quarter for reading and spelling; 2/2 for writing; $2/9\frac{1}{2}$ for arithmetic and $11/4\frac{1}{2}$ for book-keeping and mathematics. The rates were not exorbitant, but they were high enough to exclude the great majority of youngsters.

For the totally impoverished, Edmund Rice showed an early concern and it can be said that the child was father to the man. Motivated by his own feelings of compassion and caring, and undoubtedly inspired by his mother's values and encouragement, he concerned himself with those less fortunate than himself. The leadership qualities he was to show with such immense effect in later years began to make themselves evident, and through his influence, numbers of boys from the neighbourhood often gathered at the Westcourt home. There they were given simple instruction in educational and religious matters; they could shelter in a room if the weather was wet and those of them who may have been hungry were fed. The medium used by Edmund Rice in instructing his young friends was almost certainly Irish for, according to William Tighe in his *Statistical Observations Relative to the County of Kilkenny, 1800–1801,* 'the common people seldom speak any other language and Irish was prevalent about Kilkenny'.

Indeed Irish persisted for quite a long time among those whom Tighe would class as the 'commonality', and years later Dr Kieran Marum, Bishop of Ossory, 'took steps to provide books in Irish for the religious instruction through that language of large numbers of the people in the southern portion of the diocese who knew no English, or did not know it well enough to benefit from instruction in that language'. Dr Marum had a book, *The Eternity of the Soul,* translated into Irish and this, together with an Irish catechism 'was used at, before and after Mass in the rural parishes in the Ossory diocese'. It is obvious that the informal schooling given at Westcourt was largely, if not totally, through Irish, but the significant fact is that it should have happened at all. Margaret Rice undoubtedly played a significant role in it: she was described as a woman 'of refined manners, of great strength of mind and of unostentatious piety' and these were elements which she passed on in abundance to her son.

The name of the teacher in the Moate Lane school is not on record, but it is known that the method of instruction was largely oral and that pupils were given individual attention. The days were mainly spent copying headlines set by the master and repeating what had been learned by heart, and while there is no authenticated evidence as to the number of courses taken by Edmund Rice, he very probably learned at least 'the three *R*s'. He was, according to family lore preserved by Sister Josephine (daughter of a Callan Rice who emigrated to Newfoundland in 1825) 'a quiet, studious boy who became a leader among his classmates'. Despite the crude teaching methods and even cruder condition of the school, he used his time well and may, indeed, have been happy, although one tends to have reservations when one remembers a comment made about a similar school in which Amhlaoibh O'Suilleabhain taught with his father. 'It is many a long year, straight and uneventful, my father and I spent teaching in that hovel', he wrote.

Life was not entirely dismal for the majority of people in the Callan area. Part of the Irish resilience has to do with a notable capacity for making the best of things and creating a sense of gaiety whenever the opportunity presents itself. In the Callan area there was relief through music and song, games, pattern days, fair days and the like. The Feast of St Brigid was celebrated on 1 February at a pattern in Kilbride, and the local patron, St Molua, was commemorated annually early in August at Killaloe, a mile and a half from Callan. Both offered a mixture of religion and revelry, and on the sporting scene, hurling was a game which enlivened many a Sunday.

Edmund Rice was never noted for an interest in sport, but in his youth he would have been caught up in the excitement and rivalry of hurling contests. He could not have been ignorant of the fame of one Andy Delaney on the field of play, of whom a local poet wrote: 'Here active Andy famed from pole to pole/The elastic ball to hurl from goal to goal', or of the reputation of Lord Cuffe of Desart, to whom his father paid a yearly rent of approximately £300. Lord Cuffe was a benevolent landlord, and he also was a locally renowned hurler for on his death he was paid one of the highest possible tributes when a poem in his honour was composed:

> A sigh comes from many a heart
> And tears fall on many a cheek
> At not beholding thee
> With green jacket and crimson cap
> Leading out the nimble hurlers.

On the domestic level it is easy, and probably valid, to imagine the Rices enjoying a life of quiet contentment, fulfilled in their work, comfortable in their circumstances, respected by their fellows and reaping the deeply satisfying benefits of the sharing Christian ethic which was a fundamental part of their outlook. A kitchen with a warm hearth and rush-lights burning in sockets and, after the nightly Rosary, cosy beds – all part of their day-to-day routine. They were among the relative 'haves', but they were not unaware of the plight of the utter 'have-nots'. Edmund certainly was not unaware.

When he had completed his primary schooling in Callan, it was decided that his education should continue, and he was sent to what might now be roughly classed as a commercial, or secondary, school in Kilkenny. A cousin, Maurice Rice, was living there and Edmund stayed with him. Again there are few details of this important period in his life, or of the school he attended. The House Annals of Mount Sion, Waterford, record that 'in his new sphere he had the good fortune to be placed under the care of a teacher no less learned than pious. This worthy man, deeply impressed with the truths of our holy religion, communicated the same both by word and example to his youthful pupils. In after life, Mr Rice, when speaking of this good man, always did so with respect, affection and gratitude. It cannot be doubted but the early lessons of virtue inculcated by this religious teacher had the effect of producing abundant fruit in due season.'

That is the extent of the information about Kilkenny, where Edmund Rice completed his formal education around 1779 at the age of seventeen years. After his stay there he was destined for Waterford, where his uncle, Michael Rice, was running a thriving business. His going to the busy, bustling Viking city at the mouth of the river Suir, was a further and crucial step along his fated road. There, speedy and remarkable commercial success awaited him; also love and marriage, bereavement and sorrow, and the full and astonishing blossoming of his apostolate of service.

In those days, Dublin was, after London, the second city of the Empire; it was the fifth largest in Europe and was bigger than Rome. Handel's 'Messiah' had been given its first performance in Fishamble Street's New Musick Hall in 1742, and the Irish capital had its share of social brilliance, even though the ascendancy looked to London as their cultural home. The brilliance and the opulence of the Viceregal

Lodge, the Castle and the elegant town houses of the aristocracy represented, however, only one side of the coin. The other was less attractive, and in 1796 the Frenchman, La Tocknaye, could write: 'In my week in Dublin, I have seen more mud, rags and wretchedness than in my whole life in Paris.' The same conditions existed in Waterford; there, as almost everywhere else, a yawning gap divided the rich from the poor, and Edmund Rice would desert the former to throw in his lot with the latter.

A further easing of the brutal Penal Laws was on the way, but so too was the 1798 Rebellion. Relief Acts were to come, but so too was the Act of Union. There was, as yet, no sign of an end to the grinding misery, the debasement and humiliation of a race. Potatoes and milk were the staple diet for countless numbers, and there were some who could not enjoy even these meagre luxuries. Pigs and sheep were raised to pay the rent and a significant population increase was leading to subdivision of already small holdings and to further wretchedness. In the late 1770s Arthur Young wrote in *A Tour of Ireland*: 'A landlord in Ireland can scarcely invent an order which a servant, labourer or cottier dares to refuse or execute. Disrespect or anything tending towards sauciness he may punish with his cane or his horsewhip with the most perfect security. . . . Landlords of consequence have assured me that many of their cottiers would think themselves honoured by having their wives or daughters sent for to the bed of their masters, a mark of slavery that proves the oppression under which such people live.'

But still Young could add that the people 'were infinitely more cheerful and lively than anything we commonly see in England'. That cheerfulness, that resilience, that indomitable Irishry, that unbreakable spirit may even have been there when Gustave de Beaumont wrote: 'Imagine four walls of dried mud (which the rain, as it falls, easily restores to its primitive condition) having for its roof a little straw or some sods; for its chimney a hole cut in the roof, or very frequently the door through which alone the smoke finds an issue. One single apartment contains father, mother, children and sometimes a grandfather or a grandmother. There is no furniture in the wretched hovel; a single bed of straw serves the entire family. In the midst of all lies a dirty pig, the only thriving inhabitant of the place, for he lives in filth.'

Scenes of such vivid horror were witnessed by Edmund Rice all through his life and their terrible prevalence cannot be overstressed, because it was in a world composed of similar scenes that he, by mature and conscious decision, chose to live. His choice was reminiscent of St Francis of Assisi, who turned his back on wealth, social graces and fine clothes to don the rags of a beggar and embrace suffering with the sick and the poor.

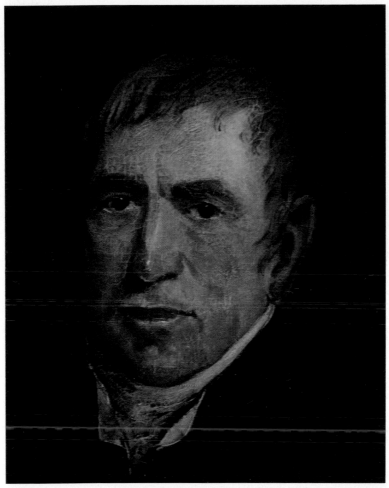

Portrait of Edmund Rice (*J. T. Dunne*)

Two views of the City of Waterford in 1824 by William Henry
Brooke

3

Success and Tragedy

The decade beginning 1780 was extraordinarily eventful for
Edmund Rice: it would alter totally the course of his life. A
newcomer to both Waterford and commercial life, he would
quickly become an outstandingly successful businessman,
respected and admired throughout the city. He would also
meet, love and marry a well-to-do girl and become the father
of a child. He would see the deaths of his wife and his father,
and he would experience the anguish of learning that his baby
daughter was handicapped. It was a decade which brought
equally remarkable shares of business advancement and personal tragedy, and from its mixture of success and suffering,
he would emerge a mature man of twenty-eight years with an
intention, as yet ill-defined, of dedicating himself to the service of God and his underprivileged fellows.

Waterford was a very prosperous centre of activity when
Edmund Rice arrived there in 1779. Its port, said to be second
only to Hamburg in the extent of its facilities, was extremely
busy and handled as many as a thousand vessels a year. In
1774 Charles Smith described it in *The Ancient and Present State
of the County and City of Waterford* as follows:

> The Quay is about half-a-mile in length and of considerable
> breadth, not inferior but rather exceeds the most celebrated
> in Europe. To it the largest trading vessels may conven-
> iently come up, both to load and to unload, and at a small
> distance opposite, they may lie constantly afloat.
>
> The Exchange, Custom House and other public
> buildings ranged along the Quay are no small addition to
> its beauty. ... The whole is fronted with hewn stone, well
> paved and in some places it is forty feet broad. To it are

built five moles or piers which stretch forward into the river; at the pier-heads ships of 500 tons may load and unload and lie afloat. In the road before the Quay the river is between four and five fathoms deep at low water, where sixty sail of ship may ride conveniently, clear of each other in clean ground.

The most substantial part of the business was with England, but there was also much trading with the Continent and, surprisingly, there was an extensive traffic with Newfoundland. In his *Tour of Ireland* which covered the years 1776 to 1779, Arthur Young wrote that 'the number of people who go as passengers in the Newfoundland ships is amazing, 3,000 to 4,000 annually from most parts of Ireland in 60 or 70 ships. The ships go loaded with pork, beef, butter and some salt. From the 1st of January, 1774, to the 1st of January, 1775, there were exported 59,856 casks of butter, each upon an average 1 cwt. at a cost of 50/– per cask.' Many of those bound for Newfoundland were interested in the seasonal employment offered by the fishing industry, but others went to settle, and it is interesting that quite a few of the latter returned to Ireland temporarily so that they could receive the Sacraments and, above all, get married in church.

In *Franciscan Ireland*, Father Patrick Conlon, O.F.M., has written that according to a census carried out around 1763, one-third of the population of Newfoundland was comprised of Irish-speaking Catholics, and in 1784 some Waterford laymen sent a petition to the English parliament seeking permission for an Irish priest to minister there. French Franciscan missionaries were already operating in the territory, and later in 1784 Father James Louis O'Donnell, O.F.M., a native of Co. Tipperary, went as prefect apostolic, and the necessity for native speakers to make the journey back to Ireland largely disappeared.

Approximately one-third of the merchants in Waterford were Catholics, and one of them was Michael Rice, Edmund's uncle. Assisted by his two sons, Robert and Patrick, he ran a thriving business at Barronstrand Street near the Quay, and a major, and lucrative, part of it was the provisioning of ships. He also supplied the military stationed on Southern Hill overlooking the city with meat, butter, hay, straw and the like. Pork was clearly another eminently saleable commodity, for Charles Smith recorded that Waterford had cornered a greater share of the Newfoundland market than any other port and this was due, in large measure, 'to the goodness of the pork fed about this place'.

It was in this bustling environment that Edmund Rice cut his business teeth in his late teens. He made his home in the parish of Ballybricken, Trinity Without, close to Barrack Street where the parish church of the time stood. It was a humble, thatched structure called the Faha Church, because it was built on a green or, in Irish, *faiche*, and Edmund Rice went to Mass there regularly – daily when his working routine allowed him. It is obvious that his working routine involved him in travelling, for the raw materials for Waterford's commercial life often came from much further afield than either city or county. Animals were bought in Limerick, Tipperary, Kilkenny, Carlow and the midland counties for slaughtering, dressing, salting and packing, with consequent employment for considerable numbers of butchers, salters, coopers, carters and labourers.

Edmund's rise to eminence in the commercial world was, by any standards, spectacular. While details are regrettably scarce, he was patently a person of exceptional acumen and ability, and there is little doubt that he made a deep impression by the integrity and honour he displayed in his business dealings. He had, at any rate, become a well-known, accepted and esteemed member of the merchant class at a comparatively young age, and he had entree to the comfortable social circle associated with it. Of fine physique and of striking, if not particularly handsome features, he was relatively well educated, intelligent and undoubtedly destined to climb very much higher on the success ladder. He was fond of jokes and had, we are told, a keen sense of humour. His qualities manifested themselves in a strength of character which would, in any time have singled him out as an achiever and a leader.

Romance entered his life in the person of Mary Elliott. A member of a well-to-do family which operated, among other things, a tanyard, she moved in the same social circle. Little is known of her otherwise: she comes into the Edmund Rice

story as a shadowy figure and leaves it tragically four years
later. They were married in 1785 when he was twenty-three
years old, and she died as the result of an accident early in
1789, after giving birth to a premature baby. There are no
records to show the nature of the accident, and reliance must
be placed on accounts handed down. Newspapers of the time
carried very brief reports of the death, but no explanatory
details.

In a letter written in 1930, Sister Josephine Rice of the
Mercy Convent, Belvedere, St John's, Newfoundland, gave
the version which had been passed on in family tradition. She
wrote: '(Edmund) had been married to a lady of a well-to-do
family who was fond of the hunt, as most wealthy people were
in those days. When she was well-advanced with child, she
went riding and was thrown from her horse, dying as a result
of the accident. The doctor managed to save the child who
had evidently been injured by the fall and hence did not
develop normally. This was the child he provided for when he
began his work (founding the Congregation of the Irish Christian Brothers).' The death must have come as a shattering
blow to Edmund.

The baby was christened Mary Rice, and her condition
compounded Edmund's sorrow. The precise nature of her
handicap is not known, but it was obviously mental, because
in later years and while she was still alive, a Christian Brother
who had been a contemporary of her father referred to her as
'weak-headed'. In her early years she was cared for by Joan
Murphy, Edmund Rice's step-sister, at 3 Arundel Place, to
which Edmund had transferred his residence from Ballybricken, and later she was brought to the family home at
Westcourt. Little more is known of her other than that she
died in Carrick-on-Suir on 23 January 1859, and was buried
next day in the cemetary at Carrigbeg.

Adequate provision for her maintenance was, however,
made throughout the seventy years of her life, and an account
book of 1826, for instance, shows that an annuity of £16 was
then being paid for her upkeep. This may appear a miserly
sum by modern standards, but at the time it was substantial.
By comparison, a curate in a Waterford parish got an annual
stipend of £10, while many workers would have been glad to

get jobs paying less. It would be very interesting to have some first hand account by Edmund Rice, either contemporaneous or in retrospect, of his reactions to his wife's death and his daughter's handicap, but no such record exists. In this, as in many other areas, a life-long reticence about his private affairs and his personal feelings leaves the curtain drawn. But there is enough material to show that a decade which started with such glowing success and promise drew to its close on successive notes of sorrow. Little more than a year before the tragic ending of his brief marriage, his father to whom he had been deeply attached, died at Westcourt. Like many others, he too showed complete trust in his son's probity and efficiency by making him executor of his will.

More than a century after Edmund Rice had lived through the grief-laden years towards the end of the 1780s, Oscar Wilde had learned enough to write: 'Where there is sorrow there is holy ground.' Wilde discovered that an enlightened acceptance of suffering led to spiritual enrichment, and it is evident that the grievous trials Edmund Rice underwent strengthened and deepened an already vibrant sense of spirituality. Following his move to Arundel Place, his house of worship was the Big Chapel off Barronstrand Street (there was a Little Chapel in Jenkins's Lane) and, like the Faha chapel, it was of modest proportions. It was discreetly tucked away to avoid giving offence or, as a contemporary noted: 'That the better to please the Protestant clergy and government, there is that course taken that the doore of this chapple is shut up, and all services ended by the time they go to Church on ye Sabbath.'

The entrance was wide enough to admit only one person at a time, and because of its siting and construction, worshippers were never left in doubt that they suffered an inferior status. The level of tolerance, already fairly high in Waterford, was rising, but there was still a long way to go to emancipation, and many old indignities remained. Edmund Rice experienced one of them when he attended his father's funeral towards the end of 1778. The remains were removed after the traditional waking at Westcourt to Callan, but as it was not permitted for a priest to officiate at the graveside, the funeral stopped at the town's crossroads. There prayers were recited and the last blessing given before the body was interred at the southern gable of the Butler Memorial Chapel.

It was Edmund Rice's practice to begin his day by hearing Mass in the Big Chapel at 6 a.m., and he was identified as one of five who received Holy Communion frequently, if not daily. In his spiritual reading, the Bible played an important part and a copy which he used, now preserved, lists him as one of those who contributed to its publication. It was a Douay version and was apparently produced with the aid of subscriptions from clergy and laity as a Catholic alternative to the many Bibles, some unorthodox, which proselytising organisations were distributing with much liberality. His autograph appears on the title page, and on the same page there is a sample of texts which obviously appealed to him, and which give an indication of the manner in which he conducted his business life and his general philosophy. The quotations are almost entirely devoted to honesty and charity and brotherhood.

They include, for example: 'If thou lend money to any of my people that is poor, that dwelleth with thee: thou shalt not be hard upon them as an extortioner, nor oppress them with usuries'; 'He that oppresseth the poor to increase his own riches shall himself give to one that is richer, and shall be in need'; 'Give to him that asketh of thee, and from him that would borrow of thee turn not away'; 'But love ye your enemies, do good and lend, hoping for nothing thereby, and your reward shall be great and you shall be the sons of the highest for he is kind to the unthankful and to the evil'; and 'Cast away from you all your transgressions by which you have transgressed, and make to yourselves a new heart and a new spirit. . . .'

This sort of biblical exhortation appealed to Edmund Rice and influenced his actions. Around 1790 he was a member of an association of young men with the common aim of spiritual growth through week-day attendance at Mass, frequent reception of the Sacraments and the reading of spiritual books. He also became increasingly involved in practical charity.

As in other parts of the country, the gulf dividing the rich from the poor in Waterford was vast. A local newspaper gave an instance of the majority's plight when it reported: 'The winter of 1783–4 was exceptionally severe. It was a disastrous year for Waterford, due to a very severe season. Widespread poverty and suffering ensued. There was a great scarcity of food. Many people were ruined in business and financial depression resulted. Poverty and want were so acute that the discipline for Lent had to be relaxed. The times were dark and gloomy; nay, they were full of turmoil and confusion, of outrage and bloodshed.' The years 1783 to 1784 may have been exceptional for the severity of the winter, but in even the best years, there was little relief for large sections of the populace from their misery.

Charitable groups bearing the names of their founders – Wyse, Butler, Fitzgerald among them – were established, but they could do little other than help a few of the most needy. Then in 1794 a new organisation was set up to bring aid and comfort to 'distressed room-keepers' – people living alone in abject poverty and isolated in their loneliness and squalor. Edmund was active in this society and may indeed have been its founder, and through it he gained first-hand experience of conditions in the city's slum areas with their filthy hovels, listless, underfed people and their ragged, idle, uneducated children.

Now in his early 30s, he had been bequeathed his uncle's still-thriving business and his status in the commercial community was at its peak. The doors of the wealthy were open to him. He might have led a refined social life of good food and drink, elegant entertainment and pleasant manners. But when his day's work was done, he spent hours in the slums, and his companions were mainly small children whom he brought to his Arundel Place house for food and instruction in religious and secular matters.

What Edmund Rice did as a schoolboy for the less well off children around Callan, he was now doing as a wealthy merchant for the poor of Waterford, old and young. He had, quite clearly, a way with him – a charisma that was not inhibited by considerations of class or possessions. His goodness, kindness, generosity, sincerity and patience were recognised. They made an impact, and several Waterford people who knew him passed on to future generations their impressions.

So we learn that 'the poor were the chief object of his attention – in fact this wonderful sympathy for God's poor was one of his most distinctive characteristics'; we know also that 'he used to endeavour to contact wild and uncared-for boys who daily gathered around the timber stacks on the Quay. Some used to laugh and jeer at him but after a while he won over many of them and got them to attend his evening school. He carried on this work in the evenings while he devoted his attention to business affairs during the day.' He was described as 'a tall, good-looking man who took, even as a businessman, a big interest in poor boys. The people looked upon him as a gift from God. He had many friends and admirers, and was reverenced and respected beyond all others in Waterford.'

One example of his practical caring concerned two young girls called Connolly. They were orphaned, and when Edmund learned of their situation, he had them reared and educated at his own expense. Another example was Black Johnny – a negro slave boy whom Edmund saw on a ship moored at the Quay. He purchased the youth's freedom from the captain and sent him to the Presentation nuns to be baptised and educated, subsequently providing him with a small house. Black Johnny, who embarked on a successful pig-rearing project, became a noted personality in the city and when he died, was widely known for his piety.

There was also the case of the young Italian boy who turned up in Waterford by barge from Carrick-on-Suir. Drenched by rain, he was selling pictures from a pack and his English vocabulary consisted almost entirely of the word 'buy'. Edmund Rice befriended, instructed and encouraged him, evidently to excellent result, for the youth was Carlo Bianconi who went on to establish a celebrated network of horse-drawn transport, accumulate much wealth and become mayor of Clonmel. 'A tall, vigorous, somewhat austere looking man, decidedly plain in appearance but homely in manner' was Bianconi's description of his benefactor, for whom he always retained great admiration and affection.

There are many more instances of Edmund Rice's capacity

for influencing people in a practical and positive manner, and it is striking how often the influence expressed itself in spiritual renewal. His contact with the wandering poet, Tadhg Gaelach O'Sullivan, is a case in point: he first met him at the Yellow House Inn, a centre of music and poetry on the Lacken Road a few miles from Waterford, and soon O'Sullivan was a regular visitor at Arundel Place. The poet was, to use a euphemism, of irregular habits, but because of Rice's influence, his way of life was transformed. Before he died, on the steps of the Big Chapel on Spy Wednesday 1795, O'Sullivan had published a volume of deeply expressive poems titled The Pious Miscellany. Edmund Rice was among the subscribers who made the publication possible, and this is one of countless examples of how practicality and spirituality went hand-in-hand in his concern for others.

His extensive and demanding round of activities did not end with business and charity. He was also involved with the Catholic Committee of Waterford, and records show that because of his standing and reputation, many went to him for advice on their daily problems. In addition to being a friend and benefactor of the poor, he became a counsellor to the not-so-poor and also, to some degree at least, a campaigner for basic rights for Catholics.

The English parliament passed Relief Acts in 1778 and 1793 but whatever trifling measures of equality they brought, they were mean in their content and objectionably narrow in one respect. The '78 Act required the taking of an Oath of Allegiance to the English monarch; an insulting declaration against the Pope and Catholic doctrine was inherent in its construction.

Some Irish bishops were of the opinion that as the oath contained nothing contrary to faith or morals Catholics could, in conscience, take it, but others disagreed. The Catholic Committee in Waterford collected signatures protesting against the wording of the oath, and Edmund Rice was among those who entered their names at the Big Chapel in April 1792. When the Relief Act of 1793 was passed, a new and less offensive oath was substituted and the Catholic Committee decided to present an address of thanks to George III.

The document does not, significantly, include Edmund

Rice's name, and neither did he sign a petition of Waterford Catholics supporting the Act of Union. He was manifestly not in favour of half measures, or of an Ireland and its people being sucked into, and being the poor relation in, a United Kingdom. He had a higher and broader vision of his country's destiny, and he would soon make a decision as to how he could best contribute to the attainment of that destiny in human and spiritual terms.

4

Towards Mount Sion

The accident which led to the tragic death of Mary Elliott
Rice had profound and enduring results. One early and
inevitable consequence was that it forced Edmund Rice to
re-think his role in life. There is no evidence that he considered re-marrying, as his mother had done, and the
prospect of a career as rich merchant and family man had
vanished. There is ample evidence, however, that he approached the decision he would soon have to make with that
blending of spirituality and practicality which was one of his
most distinctive characteristics. That he made a quick commitment to devote himself to the service of God is not in
doubt: his dilemma was the manner in which his desire to
serve could best be expressed. In his changed circumstances
he was convinced that a religious vocation would dictate his
future, but he was unsure what course it would take. According to his custom, he sought guidance through prayer.

In later years he recounted to the Presentation Sisters in
Waterford an incident which deeply influenced him and clearly enriched further his already rich spiritual life. He was
travelling one day by coach with a friar who was obviously a
man of prayer, and that night they shared the same room in a
stop-over inn. The friar, according to the account given to the
Presentation Sisters, 'employed so much of his time, not as it
occurred to Edmund Rice in asking God for favours, but in
ejaculatory prayer and blessing God, that he asked himself
why he was not so devout to God as the friar seemed to be. He
resolved from the example set him to give himself more to
prayer and to lead a monk's life of retirement and contempla-
tion.'

Edmund Rice did indeed seriously consider such a course

of action: he would go to Rome and, after visiting the tombs of the martyrs and the catacombs of the early Christians, embrace a life of solitude by becoming a lay-brother with the Augustinians, the Order in which his younger brother John was already an ordained priest. While there is no authenticated evidence, there is a strong tradition that when he disclosed this idea to a Waterford woman she told him, with commendable directness, that he would be better employed doing in Waterford for poor boys something similar to what the Presentation nuns were doing in Cork for poor girls. It was a telling point, and its practicality would have appealed to a man who was nothing if not practical and who was becoming increasingly aware of the woeful plight of Waterford's uneducated poor. This unknown lady's comment certainly offered food for thought, and according to a record left by one of the first Christian Brothers, he had made up his mind about the future by 1793, four years after the death of his wife. In 1796 he wrote to Pope Pius VI outlining his idea and was encouraged to proceed.

A pastoral letter addressed to the clergy and laity of Waterford by the recently consecrated bishop, Dr T. Hussey, in 1797, could only have strengthened his purpose. He was extremely outspoken in calling for a firm stand 'against all attempts which may be made under various pretexts to withdraw any of our flock from the belief and practice of the Catholic religion', and he asked those to whom the pastoral was directed 'to remonstrate with any parent who will be so criminal as to expose his offspring to those places of education where his religious faith or morals are likely to be perverted'. Dr Hussey, whose interest in Catholic education was widely known, was attacking proselytism, and although his pastoral letter was denounced by some non-Catholics as intolerant and reprehensible, and by some Catholics for being imprudent, it put into words what was in the minds of many.

Actually, proselytism was a thriving business at the time. The distribution of copies of the Bible, free of charge, was part of it, but an aspect which caused widespread concern related to the schools which offered free education to poor and not-so-poor children. Liberally financed from Protestant and mainly English sources, the Diocesan Free Schools had been founded in 1570; the Royal Schools in 1608; the Erasmus Smith Schools in 1657; the Chester Schools in 1733 and the Schools of the Hibernian Society would come in 1806. Whatever the surface appearances may have been, the schools were designed as a weapon with which to destroy Catholicism in Ireland, and the system of primary education that existed was almost totally in the hands of proselytising organisations.

Their rationale was that by controlling the education of the young, massive desertions from the Catholic Church would eventually result, helped by the wholesale distribution of Bibles to the adult section. As Mr John West, a member of the Baptist Society put it in a Royal Commission Report of 1825: 'We consider that Popery is an error and, having been brought to the knowledge of the truth, (the people) will certainly not remain Roman Catholics.' Mr West's judgement of the Irish character was clearly as shallow as was his concept of the truth, but his statement put into true perspective the activities of the many groups seeking to 'educate' Irish children in the late eighteenth and early nineteenth centuries.

In any event, whatever the reaction to Dr Hussey's 1797 pastoral letter, Edmund Rice would have fully understood its message and recognised its validity. No one appreciated more than he the benefits of education, or the drawbacks of a lack of it, and as a committed Catholic, he would have looked on proselytising schools with great disfavour. If the bishop's views reinforced his own in those days of waiting and praying, so also did the work of the Presentation Sisters, the congregation which Nano Nagle had founded in Cork.

A young girl who had been schooled by the nuns in Cork came to Waterford seeking employment, and the standard of her education in secular and religious subjects so impressed the parish priest of St John's, Father John Power, that he applied to Cork for the establishment of a convent in Waterford. He was told that no members were available, but if suitable personnel came forward, they would be trained in Cork and could then found an establishment in Waterford. As it happened, two relatives of Fr Power's responded and, having made their novitiate and been professed, arrived in Waterford in September 1798. It was the year of the rebellion, and because of the unsettled state of the country, they were provided with a military escort on their journey from Cork. They opened a temporary school in Jenkin's Lane on 6 November.

Edmund Rice, a close friend of Father Power, was involved in this development. He acquired a site for the Sisters at Hennessy's Road on which a permanent convent could be erected, and he was active in speeding up the building of the convent and an adjacent school. The Sisters, now six in number, moved to Hennessy's Road towards the end of 1799, and the first Mass, at which Edmund was present, was celebrated in the convent in March 1801.

Then there was the question of the nuns' dowries. Between them they had sufficient money to produce a yearly income of £108 for the running of the complex, but only if an interest rate of ten per cent could be procured. This was considerably more than could be obtained from a commercial bank, but Edmund applied his business experience and expertise to the problem. He granted the sisters a life annuity at the necessary rate on land he purchased, and thus secured the continuance of the Presentation school. There is little doubt that this involvement heightened his interest in the apostolate of Catholic education for the poor – an interest which Bishop Hussey's pastoral letter had encouraged.

Waterford had many pay-schools around the turn of the nineteenth century. Records for 1824 show that thirty-eight such Catholic schools existed and catered for 1,550 boys and girls. The numbers of pupils ranged from three in the smallest to 160 in the largest, and the fees varied from 1½d a week to £29 a year. In the same year 107 Catholics were attending the thirty-two Protestant pay-schools in operation.

The schools were, in the main, run by individual teachers who held their classes in premises variously described as 'large house', 'thatched cabin', 'slated house', 'miserable cellar', 'commodious house' and 'miserable garrett', but whatever the circumstances there were considerably more than 1,000 children whose parents were too poor to afford even 1½d a week. If that was the position in 1824, it must have been even less satisfactory in 1800, and it was around that time that Edmund Rice finally made his supremely important decision. He had prayed much; he had consulted friends whose opinions he trusted; he had received encouragement from Pope Pius VI, and Dr J. Lanigan, Bishop of Ossory, assured him that his idea had proceeded from God. As John Shelly put it in 1863: 'He heard the voice of God, and he would obey it.'

He set about disposing of his business interests, and found a purchaser, a Mr Quan. He arranged for his step-sister, Joan Murphy, and his handicapped daughter to go to relations in Callan. Having unfettered himself of matters that might divide his attention, he set about putting his remarkable project in train. A large stable in the New Street area of Waterford had become his property following the death of his wife, and he converted this two-storey building into a school. He had the ground floor transformed into three crude classrooms and space over the stable fashioned into crude bedrooms. One of these bedrooms would replace his comfortable Arundel Place residence.

New Street was lined with fashionable town houses, and the arrival of carriages with guests for house parties was a common occurence there. The stable faced on to it, and when it was discovered that the respected Mr Rice was converting it into a place for the education of unwashed, unruly boys, there were understandable objections. One objector was a Mr Compton, a Quaker and a friend of Edmund Rice. Apart from lowering the tone of the area, he considered the opening of the school foolish and unpractical. Mr Compton argued that it was also unnecessary, and in this he was articulating the generally held view that the poor were better off without education.

There was a prevalent feeling in many parts of the world that education of the poor was both unnecessary and inadvisable, and in *An Economic History of England*, C. M. Waters referred to the general attitude. 'Is it not surprising', he asked, 'that while throughout Europe (around the time of the French Revolution in 1789) there was a wave of enthusiasm for the education of the lower classes, England steadily opposed any change?' He added that 'the new aggregation of peoples, miscalled towns, had absolutely no provision for education'. The ruling classes, perhaps fearful that educated masses would undermine their priveleged position, obviously wished to encourage illiteracy, but the yearning for knowledge was there – outstandingly so in the case of the Irish.

In his *Education Systems in Ireland*, T. Corcoran quoted a reviewer in *The Times* of London who wrote: 'The love and desire for learning among the (Irish) commonality survived. It did more than survive. It was a living, natural force at the very time when, at the close of the Napoleonic War, English national education was the despair of every thinker. The hunger and thirst after learning had survived in Ireland for a period of a thousand years.' Speaking in very much the same terms, Robert Peel told the English parliament: 'I can state as a fact within my own knowledge that the greatest eagerness and desire prevails among the lower orders in Ireland for the benefits of education', and in 1812, E. Wakefield in *An Account of Ireland Statistical and Political* recorded that he 'did not know any part of Ireland so wild that its inhabitants are not anxious, nay eagerly anxious, for the education of their children'.

Despite Mr Compton's objections and reservation, Edmund Rice was not embarking on any pie-in-the-sky project; he was responding to an ingrained and profoundly felt wish. According to later accounts, he told Mr Compton that 'the only hope of improving the lot of the poor was through education and that of himself he could not hope to effect great changes in the boys, but he felt confident with the blessing of God to be able to uplift and raise them to the status of men'. To Mr Compton and others, he may have appeared a fool and an eccentric: in reality he was a down-to-earth visionary, a practical idealist and, above all, a man motivated by love who knew precisely what he was about.

From the money the sale of his business had brought him, he converted the stable into three classrooms, in one of which was a feeding trough, and he himself moved from the elegance and comfort of his Arundel Place home to the bleak austerity of a room above the stable. It was an event which must have caused very great astonishment, and to many of his commercial associates it must have seemed incomprehensible. Here was a wealthy, forty year old man, talented, successful and influential, turning his back on a mercantile world which held out so much promise and on a social life of ease and refinement. Not alone that, here was a man with no formal training setting himself up as a teacher of Waterford's most scruffy, undisciplined and poverty-stricken boys. Edmund Rice may have had his own occasional doubts when he considered the enormity of the task he was undertaking, but if he had, he was not deterred. He had made his decision after much heart searching and many hours of prayer, and he put a serene faith in God that the future would bear fruit for those whom he loved most – the poor.

As a prospective teacher, he was required to take the Oath of Allegiance, and although it was not legally necessary, he considered it prudent to obtain a licence for his modest school from the Protestant bishop, because an unlicensed school would be liable to 'window tax'. The bishop refused the licence at first but granted it when representations were made by some prominent citizens. The law specifically forbade a Catholic 'to fund, endow or establish any school, academy or college', but Edmund ignored it, and he made the most inauspicious of starts when he opened up the New Street stable as a night school. There were only six pupils at the beginning, but it was a start, and inauspicious as it may have appeared, it was momentous in its future implications.

Soon a day school followed, and through invitation, cajolement, the use of existing pupils as intermediaries and, perhaps most of all, through his own magnetism, the three classrooms were filled. Voluntary workers came to help, but dropped out when they found the going too rough and then, from his personal funds, Edmund Rice recruited two paid assistants. But they also left, despite an offer of higher salaries, because they could not cope with charges who, it seemed, were both unteachable and unmanageable. An early crisis had arisen, and those who regarded the whole affair as a ridiculous enterprise doomed to failure now appeared to be right. They were wrong: in a development which only those convinced of the power of faith would find unremarkable, two young men arrived from Edmund Rice's native Callan.

Thomas Grosvenor and Patrick Finn were eager to consecrate their lives to God, and consulted Father John Rice, who had returned to Callan. He advised them to spend a time with Edmund before they reached a final decision: in the event, they came to New Street not merely to help in teaching, but also to join Edmund Rice in the religious congregation they knew he wished to establish. The three lived over the stable and began to follow an informal discipline of prayer, work and recreation. In a dramatic transformation, class-rooms became orderly and crowded. Indeed, so many new students came to the school that an additional small school was opened in nearby Stephen Street. Teaching was carried out in Irish and English and methods were developed by trial and error. The evolution of an amazingly enlightened educational system started to take shape.

For Edmund Rice, however, his teaching apostolate was only at a stage of germination. His sights were set on a fully-fledged Congregation, governed by traditional vows, following a complete religious discipline and recognised by the Holy See. He took a crucial step towards his end when in June 1802 he commenced to build a monastery on an elevated site in a working-class district on the southern side of Waterford. On the site had stood the little thatched Faha Chapel where he had worshipped when he first arrived in the city twenty-three years earlier, and a short distance away was the Presentation convent which he had helped bring to Hennessy's Road.

Faha Chapel had been demolished and would be replaced by a new church in Ballybricken, and the site was deeded to Edmund Rice by, among others, Dean T. Hearn, who was acting for the diocese in the absence of Bishop Hussey. The building, again funded out of Edmund's private resources, was large and comprised living accommodation and a school. There were two classrooms on the ground floor and, overhead, seven bedrooms which were small and sparsely fur-nished. They had wooden beds fitted into wall recesses; an alcove served as a wardrobe and the furniture consisted of a table and a stool.

The premises were ready for occupation within a year and on 7 June 1803 it was blessed by Bishop Hussey. Following the ceremony, Dr Hussey asked by what name it would be known, and Edmund Rice invited the bishop to choose a title. Dr. Hussey, we are told, looked around and, observing the elevation of the site and its proximity to the city, was struck by the analogy to Mount Sion and Jerusalem. 'All things considered', he is reputed to have said, 'a very appropriate name would be Mount Sion.'

5

Commitment through Vows

Shortly after Edmund Rice and his two Callan companions moved to the new monastery, they were joined by a fourth, John Mulcahy of Kilmacthomas, Co. Waterford, and because the school section was not yet completed, they walked each school day to the New Street and Stephen Street classrooms. At Mount Sion, they entered on an ordered religious life which took its pattern from the Rule that governed the Presentation Sisters. Bishop Hussey permitted reservation of the Blessed Sacrament in the monastery, a privilege which was considered unusual several decades later and which, in 1803, must have brought immense joy to Edmund Rice whose devotion to the Holy Eucharist took pride of place in his spiritual life.

Dr Hussey also brought the existence of the monastery to the notice of the Holy See. He wrote that 'some few men have been formed into a Society who eagerly desire to bind themselves by the three solemn vows of chastity, poverty and obedience under rules similar to those of the (Presentation) Sisters, and already a convent residence has been built where four holy men reside who seek approbation of their rules whenever it will be deemed advisable by the Holy See.'

In Bishop Hussey, Edmund Rice had a staunch supporter and a generous benefactor: the bishop made a will on 10 July 1803, in which he directed his executors to pay 'to each master' at Mount Sion £20 per annum, and it was added that 'Mr Rice is always included as one of the masters, his salary to be for life.' The will also secured for all time the property on which the monastery and school were built, and while the provisions were extremely welcome, Edmund Rice heard of them much sooner than he would have wished.

Some hours after he had finalised his will, Dr Hussey went on a holiday to Dunmore East, a dozen miles from Waterford, and between five and six o'clock next morning, he went for a bathe with Dean Hearn. He suffered an apoplectic fit while dressing and died without regaining consciousness. His body was taken back to Waterford for burial, and the funeral procession was the occasion of a disgraceful incident. It was 12 July, and a party of drunken soldiers returning from an Orange meeting seized the coffin and tried to throw it into the River Suir. There were violent scenes before local militia recovered the remains and escorted them to the Big Chapel, where the bishop had wished to be interred.

Dr Hussey's successor was Father John Power, who had been instrumental in having the Presentation convent opened in Waterford. Like his predecessor, he was a champion of Catholic education, and he had a close and affectionate relationship with Edmund Rice. His first official act after his consecration on 25 April 1804 was to bless the now completed classrooms at Mount Sion, and the pupils from New Street were transferred there on 1 May. Henceforth Edmund could devote his undivided attention to creating the best possible educational system which the circumstances would allow.

Uncommon problems had to be faced. Edmund had relatively little experience and no training as an educationalist and special measures were patently needed to cater for the illiterate poor with whom he was dealing. Many of them were at a comparatively advanced age and many were severely lacking in discipline. Commonsense and compassion were two of the major elements Edmund applied in his approach, and in arranging an established routine, he also showed an acute understanding of the peculiar needs of the situation. He also displayed a remarkable capacity to be ahead of his time.

The system introduced at Mount Sion would be expanded and refined, but from its beginning it was, above all else, rooted in practicality. Pupils were placed according to their newness and their degree of improvement. Starters were provided with ruled slates and sharp-pointed slate pencils with which to write on them, while more proficient boys had copy-books and pens. Kindness and sympathy were encouraged, and monitors were appointed to write headlines for copying and to conduct reading practices. Things were organised to maximum efficiency so that classes could carry on their work without any interference from others: those learning to write and spell were not distracted by those learning to add and subtract. Gradation, supervision and individual attention were useful innovations, and there were periodic examinations and prize-givings. Corporal punishment was reserved for very serious faults, and in later years, it is known that when a mother brought her son to Edmund Rice for punishment he told her it was against the rules and if punishment was merited, she should administer it herself.

In a move which was altogether exceptional, and years before its time, Edmund set up a lending library at Mount Sion, with books being loaned on Fridays under the supervision of monitors. 'The boys read the library books for their parents at night and on Sundays and Holy days, and instructed them otherwise when they could do it with prudence', according to a contemporary source. 'From this, through God's mercy, and goodness, much good resulted. Boys who were bound as apprentices in the city were also supplied with pious books.' Following this innovation in Waterford, a Dublin school more than a dozen years later boasted the only lending school library in the capital city. And so, in a manner which even by modern standards is quite unusual, Edmund Rice showed an astonishing appreciation of what education means in its broadest application.

From the start he left no one in any doubt that the education he was interested in was unequivocally Catholic. The three *R*s were important, and in coming years algebra, geometry, mensuration, bookkeeping, navigation and other subjects would be added. From the first days in Mount Sion, however, there was a strong emphasis on religious instruction. He saw a knowledge of, and a dedication to, religion as an essential element for his pupils and through them, he hoped their illiterate parents would also benefit. Instruction was not enough: practice was also necessary and the boys were given ample opportunity and exhortation. Classes were interrupted at stated times for prayer, and everything possible was done to foster devotion to Christ in the Eucharist and to the Blessed Virgin Mary.

School opened at nine o'clock each morning and closed at midday with the recitation of the Angelus and Acts of Faith, Hope and Charity. Afternoon classes commenced at 1 p.m., and concluded at 3 p.m. with the litany of the Blessed Virgin, the Salve Regina and other prayers. A custom became established that every time the school clock struck the hour, work would cease, the pupils would bless themselves and say the Ave Maria. It was arranged that the boys would go to Confession and Communion at least four times a year, and a half hour was devoted each day to an explanation of the catechism.

And of this half hour, Edmund Rice wrote in a letter: 'I hold it to be the most salutary part of the system; it is the most laborious to the teachers; however, if it were ten times what it is, I must own we are amply repaid in seeing such a reformation in the children.' It was a comment of much frankness and sincerity and, almost two hundred years after it was made, its wisdom and relevance may be ignored but are in no way diminished.

Edmund Rice's preoccupation with the spiritual development of his pupils was a reflection of his own interior life. His devotion to Christ in the Holy Eucharist was total, and whatever difficulties arose – and they were both many and formidable – he took them with him to the community oratory. There he found an abundance of comfort, guidance and strength, and in living a life of faith, he set an example which was not lost on his pupils. A visiting writer, J. Bicheno, noted this in his book, *Ireland and Its Economy* when he wrote: 'There was frequent attendance in the chapel within the walls of the schoolhouse. Great stress was laid upon a regular appearance at Mass and at Confession, and the priests were very attentive to the pastoral charge of the young.'

Similarly, Rev. Dr Corcoran, S.J., commented that the Rice school regulations, fully developed by 1810, 'are of great value as showing how the traditional hedge-school practice concerning religious instruction and the basic school arts was standardised and improved for use in the new and larger Catholic urban schools. This was done on entirely Irish lines.'

The system devised by Edmund Rice developed so that it embraced a graded educational programme from the lowest primary level to a complete secondary training. It was immensely practical as well as being uncompromisingly religious, and from the earliest days at Mount Sion, the practicality was obvious in the way the boys responded to their schooling. The change in their behaviour and in their capabilities was widely noted and, in a related area, the depth of Edmund Rice's extraordinary kindness, compassion, caring and sensitivity made a profound impression on people of all religious persuasions.

The items necessary to the boys' education – writing requisites, books and the like – were supplied free of charge, but things went much further. A bake-house was erected at Mount Sion so that the hungry would have bread, and over it a tailoring workshop was set up. To it were brought large quantities of clothing materials to be made into suits, coats and trousers for the needy, and if the Mount Sion library was before its time, this work was even more striking in its quintessential Christianity. Records show that in 1813, 365 yards of ratteen (a type of tweed manufactured in Carrick-on-Suir) were purchased at 3/– a yard; 286 yards of dowlas (a coarse calico) at 1/4 a yard; 181¾ yards of corduroy at 3/– a yard and 262 yards of linen at 1/7 a yard. One tailor was in constant employment, and on occasions as many as seven were hired on a part-time basis.

The clothing made in the workshop was given to those who needed it, when they came to class, when they made their first Holy Communion or when they were leaving to take up employment, and in all cases Edmund Rice showed a remarkable delicacy in his appreciation of the feelings of people who, however poor, had their dignity. Shoes were also provided, and old records include such entries as: 'stockings for an orphan, 2/–; coat for a boy going to a trade, 8/–; shoes for boys in the kitchen, £1–14–0; shoes for Daniel and Michael S, 9/10; for making 95 coats and 91 trousers, £9–6–0; for making 42 suits and trimmings, £4–8–9'.

This beautiful aspect of Mount Sion was commented upon by Mr and Mrs S. C. Hall in *Ireland, Its Scenery and Character* when they wrote: 'The most destitute of the children are clothed – but in such a way that their dress does not distinguish them from the other scholars. . . . Boys leaving school for situations are, when in need of it, provided with decent and comfortable clothes. . . . Boys making their first Holy Communion were provided with good clothes in honour of the event and afterwards were brought to Mount Sion and given breakfast.'

The effects of Mount Sion's mixture of practicality, humanity and spirituality were clearly apparent to the people of Waterford, and the school attracted so many pupils that eventually extra space had to be provided. Temporary sheds were erected in the playground, and benches on which the boys could sit were borrowed from a nearby publican. They were carried to the sheds each morning and returned in the afternoon, and it was obvious that further permanent accommodation was needed. In 1816, an extension project had to be abandoned because of lack of funds, and an advertisement appealing for financial support was published in the *Waterford Chronicle* and the *Waterford Mirror*. It referred to 'the necessity of refusing admittance to several hundred poor children who have been making application these three or four years past', and stated that £250 was required to complete the scheme.

In a supporting editorial, the Chronicle stated that Mount Sion had 'withdrawn multitudes from the dangers of idleness and vice and has reared them in the pursuit of useful knowledge and in habits of virtuous and honourable industry. . . . A general confidence is placed in the character of those who have been educated and merchants, trades etc. are anxious to have them in their employment, relying implicitly on a faithful and undeviating discharge of their duties.' It added that instruction was given annually to 'about 600 persons, 200 of whom, through want of accommodation, have received this tuition in the open air'. The appeal was successful: it brought in a sum of £310 and the desired classrooms were completed and furnished.

There is no record of the amount received by Edmund Rice from the sale of his business interests, but it must have been substantial. He paid for the erection of the Mount Sion buildings – approximately £3,000 – out of liquid assets, and he invested a considerable sum in land and property. At the time he started his apostolate, he owned 140 acres of land in Co. Kilkenny, the Garter Inn in Callan and ten dwelling houses in Waterford. Bequests and contributions he also invested, and the income accruing from all sources was devoted exclusively to his educational and charitable activities. It was never enough, however, to meet all the demands and as in the case of the extension to Mount Sion, lack of finance would be a recurring and painfully restrictive factor when other schools were established elsewhere.

But whatever the monetary difficulties, the object of founding a Congregation remained very much in the forefront: the apostolate of Catholic education was needed even more in other parts of the country than in Waterford, and only through the recruitment of disciples could the desired expansion take place. A Congregation with the full backing of Papal authority would go a long way towards achieving this, and it would also enable a religious life to be lived to its spiritual fullness.

The official attitude towards Catholics was far from ideal or even acceptable, but it had mellowed and was markedly better than it had been in the eighteenth century. Proselytism remained rampant, but the repressive campaign had eased, perhaps because the British parliament was concerned with weighty matters elsewhere. 'We are disputing about catechisms while Napoleon is conquering kingdoms', a politician told the House of Commons.

In Waterford, there was a growing tendency towards liberalisation among enlightened Protestants, and the work of Edmund Rice and his colleagues was probably a factor. Edmund had a number of non-Catholic friends and one of the closest and most influential was Sir John Newport who represented the city in parliament for many years.

In 1808 a group of prominent Waterford Protestants passed a resolution in which they stated that 'they knew no reason why all the benefits of the British constitution should be any longer withheld from so large a portion of His Majesty's faithful and loyal people, and that a measure of emancipation will eventually contribute to the harmony, security and stability of the British empire'. It went on: 'We feel ourselves called on respectfully, but clearly, to declare our decided conviction that the longer continuance of these restrictive laws would be unjust and impolitic. . . . It is our earnest wish that these unhappy divisions and lines of demarcation be obliterated for ever.' Following this heartening Waterford lead, Protestants in Kilkenny, Clare, Limerick and Tipperary adopted similar resolutions.

Edmund Rice's ambition to establish a Congregation was in direct contravention of the law as it stood, but he was already in contempt of the statutes through the founding of Mount Sion and he was not unduly worried by taking the contempt a stage further. With the agreement of Bishop Power, he and his companions decided to wait no longer: they would set up a Congregation, however informal, by binding themselves to the traditional vows in a ceremony of religious profession.

This they did on a day specially chosen – 15 August, the feast of the Assumption of the Blessed Virgin, 1808. There were seven involved, and after hearing Mass in the Presentation convent, they 'made annual vows according to the rule and constitution of the Presentation Order as approved by the Holy See in the presence of Right Rev. John Power'. It was an historic occasion and a day of great rejoicing for Edmund Rice and his followers. They had been leading a life governed by poverty, chastity and obedience, and a commitment to educating the poor, but now they had made a solemn act of consecration in the presence of and with the blessing of the local representative of the Holy See.

The taking of annual vows was, however, only a step towards the eventual goal. Bishop Power wrote to the Pope praising the work being done and stating that he 'anxiously recommends to Your Holiness the ardent desire and petition of the pious and devoted laymen to obtain an Apostolic Brief similar to that previously granted to the nuns of the Presentation Order, which would grant the faculty of making simple vows so that their charitable work may be canonically sanctioned'.

The reply received from the Holy See could not have been more encouraging. Cardinal Pietro, Prefect of the Sacred Congregation, wrote that the request 'has brought much consolation' and that 'the zeal and religious disposition of these devout men are highly praiseworthy'. He asked that the rules and constitutions by which the new Institute would be governed be forwarded and 'after the same have been examined and approved, the desired Brief will be obtained'.

The community moved closer to their goal on 15 August 1809 when, after an eight-day retreat, and again in the presence of Dr Power, they made perpetual rather than annual vows. On this occasion they also pledged themselves to the charitable instruction of poor boys and each adopted a religious name. Edmund Rice became Brother Ignatius after the Spanish *hidalgo*, Ignatius Loyola, who founded the Society of Jesus and led the counter reformation movement with a degree of piety, zeal and self-sacrifice that astonished most of Europe. The proselytising campaign in Ireland has been called the Second Reformation, and if this is a valid description, it can be said of Brother Ignatius that his role in the Second Counter Reformation was not dissimilar to that of Ignatius Loyola in the first.

6

School and Jails

To the public generally, Brother Ignatius always remained Mr Rice during his lifetime, and he and those who joined him were for many years collectively referred to as 'the monks'. They were also known as the Brothers of the Christian Schools before members of their Institute, or Congregation, eventually established their name all over Ireland and in many parts of the world as the Irish Christian Brothers. As will be seen later, the Presentation Brothers, too, owe their origin to Edmund Rice and look upon him as an immensely reverend founder.

He was a man of exceptional stamina with seemingly endless reserves of physical strength, a strength which appeared to become ever more freshly renewed the more austere life became and the more daunting the difficulties, heart-aches, rebuffs and sorrows that arose. He was described as 'above middle height, being about six feet tall, and of a ruddy complexion with eyes large and expressive and of a light hazel colour, and hair sandy or brown. He was of athletic build and his intellectual powers were of the highest.' He had remarkable leadership qualities and his name was a household word among the people 'as a saintly man raised up by God for the good of his people and to do a great work'. He appeared to all 'as one sent by God to fulfil a special mission, and that mission was that he came to his people and to the Church at a time when they were in need of such a man, and his fame soon spread outside the limits of Waterford'.

He was a man of dispassionate passion insofar as he was consumed by a love which was intense and transcendental but which was expressed with a tranquility of mind that was altogether lacking in extrovertive or demonstrative elements.

If people felt obliged to describe him as one sent by God – and they were many – they did so because they recognised an aura of sanctity springing from a deep well, and not because of any image-building or credit-seeking action on the part of the man himself.

Life in Mount Sion was patterned on a severe regimen. The Brothers rose at 5 a.m., and the day was divided between prayer, teaching, private devotion, study and recreation. They ate only two meals: there was a breakfast of bread, butter and milk at around 8 a.m., and dinner, plain and mostly meatless, was at 3.30 p.m. Brother Ignatius is known to have used instruments of penance, such as the hair shirt, as a further enriching agency, and while it may appear that the routine was physically debilitating and not all conducive to leading a life crammed with demanding activity, it in no way lessened his keen enthusiasm for helping others.

He was utterly inexhaustible in expanding the range of his concern. He taught in Mount Sion and he looked after the administrative side of a school catering for several hundred pupils. He supervised the making and distribution of bread and clothes, and the demands made by these duties would have been sufficient to keep any ordinary person fully occupied. Brother Ignatius was not ordinary, however: there were no deprived or suffering people to whom his compassion did not reach out in abundance, and he involved himself eagerly and willingly in a variety of works which were time-consuming and, in many instances, grim.

Worried about parents of his pupils, their illiteracy and their lack of religious instruction, he set up evening classes at Mount Sion, and they were well attended. He introduced a Sunday morning school and it too flourished. He also found time to spend with prisoners in Waterford's city and county jails.

Popular middle class attitudes towards the lower classes placed little official emphasis on human life and none at all on human dignity. The condition of prison inmates was extremely harsh, and the penalty for petty theft, as for political offences, was often execution by hanging. That apart, a Government report stated that 'the young delinquent is soon converted into a hardened criminal . . . the most effective teachers of depravity, bad example and evil communications are in uninterrupted action.' Brother Ignatius embraced this horrific scene in his apostolate, and regularly made his way to the jails with some of his companions to give instruction, to disburse money for prisoner comforts and to bring a measure of consolation and courage to those serving sentences, especially to those awaiting execution.

Public hangings were not uncommon, and in 1799 Edmund Rice had witnessed the execution of a nephew of his friend, Dean Hearn. Francis Hearn was a clerical student approved for ordination when he was accused of being connected with the United Irishmen. He was sentenced to death, and hanged on the bridge outside the county jail. Following a barbaric custom, his body was left dangling on the scaffold for some hours before it was surreptitiously cut down and dropped into the River Suir. A number of men, who were in a boat hidden under the bridge, retrieved the remains and took them away to a lonely spot for waking and burial.

A year earlier he had saved one of his own kinsmen from a similar fate. John Rice of Newlands, Co. Kilkenny, was known locally as 'the wild rapparee', and probably took part in the '98 rebellion. In an effort to capture him, yeomen surrounded his house and, having failed to find him, burned it down. Rice managed to make his way to Waterford and was subsequently smuggled in a barrel on a ship bound for Newfoundland. Edmund had hidden him in his house and arranged his escape: both were capital offences, but as he had complete freedom of movement on the Quay, he was not suspected.

He became a regular visitor to the jails, and one account book recorded that on Christmas Day, 1807, he disbursed £5–13–9 to prisoners – a half-crown to each of forty-two – and he clearly used the Irish system of currency which, at the time, gave the half-crown a value of $2/8\frac{1}{2}$. This was a practical aspect, but he saw these visits as fulfilling an infinitely more valuable purpose. Spiritual renewal was his primary aim, and he concentrated particularly on the condemned so that they might, he hoped, face death with a degree of serenity and resignation. It is recorded that many under sentence had become so hardened and bitter that they rejected approaches made by prison chaplains, but mellowed under the influence of Edmund Rice and his fellow Brothers.

On the mornings of executions, Edmund was granted the special privilege of meeting the condemned, spending the last couple of hours with them, and accompanying them to the scaffold. This became an established practice over the years, and in 1912 Thomas Burke of Yellow Road, Waterford, then aged 86, recalled having seen a public execution in 1836 when he was ten years old. He had a vivid recollection of seeing the condemned man being helped on to the scaffold by a priest and a Christian Brother, and his statement was later verified through a news item in *The Dublin Pilot* of 23 March 1836. The paper reported that 'on Saturday, 19th inst., two men were executed in front of the county prison . . . preparations for the removal of the convicts commenced a little before noon and they were soon seen to proceed along the passage accompanied by the Reverend Timothy Dooley and two Brothers of the Christian Schools. . . . The Brothers of the Christian Schools at Mount Sion were ever to be found where they can administer comfort and alleviation in such circumstances, and they were assiduous in their exertions from the time the men left the dock after their conviction.'

In stark contrast to prevailing attitudes, Brother Ignatius turned his efforts undeviatingly towards the poor. The more wretched, down-trodden and suffering they were, the more he applied himself to their cause. About the founding of his first school, it was said of him that he saw a soul in every poor child, and Christ in every soul. Poor children were and would remain his special concern, but the comment was equally relevant to all the poor, irrespective of age. Wherever poverty and need were most acute, he was there.

One instance of the scope of his work can be found in his involvement with the Association for the Suppression of Mendicity, a society set up in the early 1820s. Bad weather, crop failure and a partial famine had caused very great hardship. Farmers who could not pay their rent were evicted, and homeless families swarmed into Waterford. The streets were full of beggars, and of the many who called at Mount Sion for food, none was turned away. When one Brother complained

Edmund Rice's house, Arundel Place, Waterford (*J. T. Dunne*)

Edmund Rice's house at Westcourt (*J. T. Dunne*)

that supplies were on the point of exhaustion, Brother Ignatius told him: 'God will send us enough.'

The Haliday Pamphlets gave a description of the conditions in Waterford: 'Many of the mendicants, themselves the victims of disease, carried about with them the seeds of infection. . . . Others displayed to open view the ravages of the most loathsome distempers and sought for relief by an appeal from which every delicacy recoiled with horror, while the young were trained up by their parents in the same paths of moral ruin.' The Association for the Suppression of Mendicity rented a three-storey house which became known as the Mendicity Asylum, and street beggars were compelled to report to it every morning.

They were given a meagre breakfast and while the men were then sent to sweep the streets and, later, to grind oyster-shells and limestone as a top-dressing for land, the women were put to work making sacks, mats and mops for sale. The Asylum closed at nightfall, and the inmates had to find whatever lodgings they could with the money given them – $2\frac{1}{2}$d a week per person, or 5d for a family. Despite teaching at Mount Sion, holding evening classes, conducting Sunday school and visiting jails, Brother Ignatius found time to devote to the Association, and his participation must have been considerable, for he was one of the few Catholics appointed to its board of management and he was subsequently elected its chairman. As was his wont, he and some other of the Brothers attended to instruct the Catholic men and boys in preparation for the reception of the sacraments. Considering the range of activities and the physical demands entailed, it is not altogether surprising that a novice at Mount Sion at the time should have noted that Brother Ignatius was so tired when the day ended with the recitation of the Rosary, he placed pebbles under his knees to keep himself awake.

'The whole atmosphere of Mount Sion was glowing with his presence', a Brother stated. 'Novices who entered heard of his many virtues, above all his great spirit of prayer, of his remarkable charity, of his spirit of reverence which showed itself in his attitude towards all things concerned with the worship of God, his great respect for the mysteries of religion and his unhesitating submission to spiritual authority. It was the prudence, the almost inspired foresight, the charity, the forbearance, the enlightenment, all of which were the fruits of silent prayer before the tabernacle, that enabled him to steer the bark of the Institute through all the turbulent waters of the early years.'

Turbulent the early years most certainly were. Brother Ignatius would, among other things, face vilification from highly-placed Catholic clerics; charges against him over forged signatures; appalling financial problems and insults directed at him and his Institute by non-Catholics. But he would pursue his course with doggedness and equanimity.

That criticism should come from Protestant sources was inevitable, for he was seriously hindering proselytism. H. D. Inglis was typical in *A Journey Through Ireland*. He wrote: 'The most important institution I visited (in Waterford) was a Catholic school at which upwards of seven hundred children were instructed . . . and although I am far from questioning the motives of either the founder, Mr Rice, or of the young men who thus made a sacrifice of themselves, yet I cannot regard favourably an institution under such tuition. I know too much of Catholicism in other countries to doubt that intellectual training will be made very secondary to theological instruction . . . I would rather not see a system of education extensively pursued in which the inculcation of Popish tenets forms the chief feature.'

Mr Inglis was obviously worried, and had reason to be, if he found the inculcation of Popish tenets objectionable, but he was much less acerbic than a contributor to the *First Report of the Commission on Irish Education*: 'The plan of education pursued in the schools is perhaps the most intolerable and mischievous which any individual or society has attempted to mask under the disguise of Christian instruction, and nothing could be more hopeless in a human sense, than the task of attempting to eradicate the peculiar impressions which are burned into juvenile feeling by the operation of the system. There are about 6,000 orthodox larvae in these poisonous receptacles, and the queen bee, it seems, is still in vigorous operation.'

This strange comment with its curious metaphor came at a

time when several Christian Brothers' schools were thriving, and Brother Ignatius's sense of humour would have been tickled by the description of him as 'the queen bee'; but despite the display of deep-seated, anti-Catholic prejudice, the report did concede that 'the children are kept in good order and the masters seldom have recourse to corporal punishment'.

Had he needed non-Catholic praise, Brother Ignatius got it in generous measure from interesting sources. The Reverend R. H. Ryland, Dean of Christ Church Cathedral, wrote in 1824: 'In the schools established by Edmund Rice, Esq., for the education of poor Catholic children, we have a splendid instance of the most exalted generosity. . . . Among a distressed and unemployed population, where religious opinions militate against the system of education offered them by their Protestant brethren, these schools have been of incalculable benefit: they have already impressed upon the lower classes a character which hitherto was unknown to them, and in the number of intelligent and respectable tradesmen, clerks and servants which they have sent forth, bear the most unquestionable testimony to the public services of Edmund Rice.'

A few years later, Sir John Newport, M.P., writing on behalf of himself, the mayor of Waterford and 67 prominent citizens, gave equally enthusiastic and understanding commendation: 'The schools established by Mr Edmund Rice', he wrote, 'and which up to this date have continued, and still continue, to afford every opportunity to hundreds of poor children of this city to acquire a truly useful education, have materially contributed to improve the morals of our youth, by the excellent system of instruction which is practised in them, and to diffuse among our poor principles of integrity and social order. I have the highest possible opinion of the system of instruction pursued in Mr Rice's Waterford school, and have for many years witnessed with the most cordial satisfaction the infinite benefits resulting from it to the inhabitants of this city in particular and to the public generally.'

According to the comments of Dean Ryland and Sir John Newport, Mr Rice was a 'queen bee' of undoubted value: he would, in any event, persevere with his apostolate whatever

the criticism or the praise; whatever the obstacles or the encouragement. He would need his faith, his perseverance and
his sense of humour.

   To a solicitor who chided him for not having spoken to him
when they had passed each other in the street the previous
day, he replied that he was afraid to speak in case 'it would
mean another 6/8'. That was typical of his droll humour, and
more instances were doubtless shown when the Mount Sion
community, 'very happy and united' in spite of the pressures
of work, held their occasional festive entertainments. Brother
Ignatius, we are told, would join in and sing his favourite
Moore's melody: 'Oh! had we some bright little isle of our
own/In a blue summer ocean, far off and alone. . . .' Such
hours of felicity were, however, brief.

7

Spreading Branches

The rapid and dramatic improvement in the conduct and capabilities of the poor boys from Waterford's slums as a result of their education at Mount Sion was noted by all sections of the community, and inevitably news of the transformation spread to other areas. Educational facilities, and especially facilities with a Catholic orientation, were hopelessly lacking in scores of towns, and this was a cause of much concern to bishops, priests and a significant number of laity. In seeking a solution, the growing reputation of Mount Sion impressed them; the disciplined blending there of the practical and the spiritual offered the ideal answer, particularly when the achievements of the system were reported in glowing terms. Consequently, increasing numbers turned to Mount Sion with requests for the establishment and staffing of schools.

Edmund Rice was never exclusively interested in Waterford's illiterate poor. His apostolate recognised no boundaries; his spirit of caring and sharing was all-embracing and it reached out to all people in need, irrespective of geographical, ethnic or other considerations. From the beginning, he had a vision of a Congregation of men as dedicated as himself who would go forth to raise boys out of their ignorance and misery, to give them dignity and the capacity to engage in useful, satisfying employment and, above all, to appreciate the full richness of their Catholic heritage. He did not, perhaps, foresee the extraordinary world-wide growth of the movement to which he pledged himself, but he was acutely conscious of the need for it in the Ireland of his time, and he was aware that without attracting postulants nothing much could be achieved. The Papal Brief would help because it would bring the ultimate in canonical endorsement, but before it came, many fruitful seeds from Mount Sion would have been planted in other areas of Ireland.

The first offshoot from the parent house was in Carrick-on-Suir. A rich wine merchant, Thomas Brien, financed the erection of a monastery on a plot of ground on the main road to Waterford, donated by a local gentleman, Terence Doyle, and a school was built by public subscription. One classroom was ready for occupation on 6 January 1806, and John Mulcahy was appointed by Bishop Power, on Edmund Rice's recommendation, to lead a community which consisted of himself, Mr Brien and William Hogan of Clerihan. H. D. Inglis described Carrick as 'distinguished in nearly equal proportions by the exquisite oppulence and soft beauty of the sumptuous valley which forms its environs, and by the haggard misery, the squalid poverty, the pinched and starving distribution of employment which characterise the great body of its population. I was struck with its deserted falling-off appearance . . . and with the very poor, ragged population that lingered about the streets.'

The Carrick foundation had a disastrous start. Sixty boys described as 'rude, ignorant and uncultivated' presented themselves on the opening day and were crammed into a room measuring thirty feet by twenty. Despite his experience at Mount Sion, John Mulcahy could not maintain control and Thomas Brien, with no experience at all, was of no assistance. The boys were brought under some kind of control by local curates, but it was a number of days before the school could operate normally. Edmund Rice always had a special affection for the Carrick foundation, partly because it was the first offshoot from the parent stem and partly because of the challenge it presented. For several years its survival was in doubt owing to lack of money, and in 1816 an order for its closure was made but not implemented because a man of doggedness and courage, Patrick Corbett, arrived on the scene.

Towards the end of 1807, a foundation was opened in Dungarvan where conditions were somewhat similar to those in Carrick-on-Suir. The town, according to Inglis, was 'edificed with wretched houses and hovels, irregular in the alignment of its streets and filthy in its thoroughfares'.

Despite his unimpressive debut in Carrick, John Mulcahy was appointed director, and he was joined by his elder brother, James, who had entered Mount Sion a short time previously. They took up temporary lodgings and set up school in a disused store, and the opening day augured well. 'More than two hundred boys swarmed into the classroom, none of whom had previously attended any school', but the financial difficulties were severe. Interest on a bequest of £1,000 from William Barron of Faha, Co. Waterford, was the only source of revenue, and the Mulcahy brothers took up part-time farming to supplement the revenue.

The next extension was in Cork, a city with a population of eighty thousand, a thriving commerce and a large export trade. Here again the gap between the poor and the rich was vast and, while suburbs like Montenotte, Tivoli and Blackrock had comforts, refinements and elegance, there were also warrens of mud-walled cabins in areas subject to frequent outbreaks of diseases like typhoid and typhus, caused by overcrowding, pollution, contaminated water and hunger. For the better-off children there were many pay-schools, but for the poor the facilities were grossly inadequate, even though Nano Nagle had set up five free schools for girls and two for boys, and even though the Cork Charitable Society, formed in 1793 to provide education for the poor, was running eleven schools catering for approximately 750 pupils.

In 1807 the Charitable Society began work on two schools with accommodation for two hundred and six hundred boys respectively, but despite these endeavours, the position remained altogether unsatisfactory, largely because of the inefficiency of the teachers employed. The Bishop of Cork, Dr F. Moylan, had heard of Edmund Rice's Mount Sion enterprise as early as 1804 and some years later he visited Waterford, inspected the school and interviewed Edmund. Evidently impressed, he asked for some Brothers to go to Cork.

No members of the Mount Sion community could be spared, but Edmund Rice said he would receive aspirants from Cork and return them on completion of their training, which was exactly what had happened, in reverse, in the case of the arrival of the Presentation nuns in Waterford. The idea was accepted and on 17 March 1810, Jerome O'Connor and

John Leonard arrived at Mount Sion to begin their spiritual
formation under the direction of Brother Ignatius. After taking their vows, they returned to Cork in November 1811, and
started their teaching mission in a school assigned to them in
Chapel Lane. It was an existing educational establishment,
and to their dismay, they found two lay teachers openly quarrelling while the pupils were 'so grossly ignorant and immoral
that the most profane language was used by them in the hearing of the Brothers'.

The Brothers occupied a temporary monastery early in
1812, and were tremendously encouraged when, within two
years, they were joined by four mature aspirants, including
Patrick Joseph Leonard, then aged 29 and a native of
Doneraile. By the end of 1816, a permanent monastery and
school had been erected at Fair Hill at a cost of £5,000 collected by the Charitable Society. It became known as the
North Monastery.

Conditions in Cork delayed the opening of the school.
Because of bad weather, food was so scarce that shops were
frequently looted. The Brothers lived on two meals a day of
potatoes and milk, and meat was an unknown luxury. One
member of the community, Brother Ignatius McDermott,
died of what was described as 'the decline' and in a typhus
epidemic an estimated 25 per cent of the city's population
died. The Cork Historical and Archaeological Society's journal recorded that 'the fever continued at such an alarming increase that the usual fever houses could not contain one-half
of the cases. The monks, to their credit, gave up a large
building of theirs intended for a school-house, and it was
opened for the reception of patients.' Another Brother,
Jerome Francis Ryan, died of the disease.

The North Monastery school eventually opened, and the
classification of pupils on admission shows how the Rice
educational system had evolved: 'there were 210 for spelling
and reading; 200 for arithmetic; 20 for geometry and mensuration; 20 for book-keeping and 67 for trade appren-
ticeships'. The routine established in Mount Sion as regards
prayer and religious instruction was an integral part of the
system.

During the time Edmund Rice was training the Cork

postulants, a request came from Dr Daniel Murray, coadjutor
to the Archbishop of Dublin, Dr John Thomas Troy, asking
for the establishment of a school in the capital. Dublin had a
Catholic population of more than 200,000, but the education
of youth was almost entirely in the hands of Protestants.
There were 48 Catholic schools catering for 1,300 boys. Of
these only eight were free, and they had a capacity for no
more than 255. Facilities for Catholic education of the poorest
children were extremely bad.

Mount Sion reacted gladly to Dr Murray's request, and
two Brothers were sent to Dublin in the early months of 1812.
They took up temporary residence at Moira Place, fairly close
to the school premises in Hanover Street. The school served a
dockland area where 'the lanes and streets are filled with filth:
there are no sewers, no attention is paid to the ventilation of
the houses and the poor are obliged to buy even the water
which they drink: it is of the worst description and tends to
promote disease as much by its scarcity as by its quality. The
sufferings of the poor from want of fuel, want of water and of
clothing can only be credited by those who witnessed them.
The sufferings of the poor children cannot be described; many
perish and those who survive are, in many instances, so
debilitated by want as to become sickly and infirm at an early
period of life.'

This was the sort of scene which Edmund Rice and his followers often witnessed; these were the circumstances in which
their apostolate could find its most abundant outflowing.
When he visited the Hanover Street school in 1813, Edmund
was clearly dismayed, not so much by the poverty and the
wretchedness as by the inadequacy of the amenities and the
difficulties of the financial situation. In a letter, he wrote that
during his visit his spirits 'were for the most part as low as
ditch water', but with his accustomed faith and acceptance he
added: 'May the will of God be done in it.' Encouraged by his
supremely Christian approach, the Brothers carried on their
teaching duties, and plunged into the extra-curricular activities for which Mount Sion was noted. They set up a Sunday school for adults and their attendance in the male wards
of Jervis Street hospital became a regular feature of Sundays
and Holy days. To the wretched young and to the equally

wretched adults, they gave themselves with a selflessness that was a basic element of Edmund Rice's inspired mission.

Thurles was another town desperately in need of free education. In a population of 7,500 there were approximately 1,200 males over the age of five years who could neither read nor write and a further 424 who could only read.

In the diocese of Cashel and Emly of which Thurles was the episcopal seat, the expanding activities of proselytising societies had been a cause of anxiety for many years, and while quite a few Catholic pay-schools were operating, the general position was considered altogether unsatisfactory by Archbishop Thomas Bray, who succeeded Dr James Butler in 1792. One school in Thurles was described in a report of 1824 to '25 as 'a miserable hovel', yet it accommodated 70 Catholic students who paid fees ranging from 1/6 to 3/4 (roughly $7\frac{1}{2}$p to 16p) a quarter, and another called 'a stable' catered for 37. Elsewhere in the diocese there were 59 pupils attending classes in 'a cow-house' and one educational institution was 'a school in a hedge over which a covering is thrown'. Eighty-four children, all Catholics, were being educated there.

The Christian Brothers established themselves in the town after two men, William Cahill of Thurles and Thomas Cahill of Callan, had undergone training and made their novitiate at Mount Sion in 1815. Thomas had been a prosperous boot-maker and the owner of a considerable property in his native Callan. He had strong nationalistic leanings. In 1790 he was arrested by yeomen, brought to the crossroads in Callan, hung from its infamous triangle and flogged almost to death. He was released at the intervention of a local Protestant gentleman.

In 1816 the Bishop of Limerick, Dr C. Tuohy, invited the Brothers to open a school. As in the case of Thurles, Limerick's need was acute: 17,000 people over the age of five were illiterate in a population of 45,000, and there was extreme poverty, especially in the Irishtown district. *The Parliamentary Gazetteer* gave an account of how bad things were in a report which stated that Limerick had 'for a considerable time the painful reputation of exceeding any other town in Ireland in the wretchedness of its inhabitants, and even if abatement should be made for some over-colouring in the dismal accounts given it by tourists and other observers, it may well be noted as furnishing the very acme of those evils of starvation, disease and putridity which render the poor sects of the Irish population so many segregations of charnel houses of the living'.

Three Brothers arrived in Limerick in June 1816, and found to their dismay that nothing had been done to provide them with either lodgings or a school. They took up temporary accommodation in Hill's Lane, Irishtown, 'a vast mass of delapidation, filth and misery', and through the doggedness of Brother Austin Dunphy, temporary school rooms were opened. Carpenters were employed to make thirty-four long desks to accommodate 408 pupils, a number which, Brother Austin drily remarked 'will give plenty to do for us three'. Again, there were dire financial difficulties, but following the lead given by Edmund Rice, it was somehow contrived to provide clothes for the worst-off of the boys. To keep a clothes fund going, the Limerick Brothers begged from door-to-door every Saturday.

A school was opened in Cappoquin in 1813, and in Ennistymon eleven years later, with classes held in a disused chapel. The foundation there was named Mount St Joseph, and one of those assigned to it was Brother Francis Manifold. He had been a Protestant and a Major with the Wicklow yeomen who converted to Catholicism and followed Edmund Rice in dedicating himself to the poor. In Ennistymon he made wheel-barrows to supplement the school's meagre income, and endeared himself so much that when he died of typhus at Ennis hospital in 1840, a large number of Ennistymon people turned up and demanded that he be returned for burial to Mount St Joseph. Huge crowds walked with the funeral the eighteen miles to Ennistymon, and many reported witnessing a remarkable phenomenon – a light like a star, but much brighter and larger, which moved along with the cortege as it approached the town. 'It was night when the funeral procession was coming into Ennistymon', an eye-witness reported, 'and a bright light over the corpse was seen for miles around until the funeral reached the monastery.'

Requests were reaching Mount Sion in increasing numbers and from greater distances, and the first venture outside

Ireland at Preston in 1825. It was followed the next year with a foundation in Manchester – the first venture in a large industrial city, where around 30,000 children, mainly Irish, were without any kind of educational facilities. A second Manchester school came later, and London became the centre of a number of foundations. At the period of its greatest expansion, the Christian Brothers' Institute had fifteen houses and seventy-three Brothers in England, but because of difficulties relating to management, finances and other matters, activity on the English scene came to a close in 1880. For similar reasons, a foundation in Gibralter during the latter part of the 1830s survived for only a year or so.

All this activity put a great deal of work, much travel and endless worry on the already heavily-burdened shoulders of Edmund Rice. Several schools at one time or another faced closure because of a shortage of money, and from the totally inadequate funds at his disposal, Edmund tried to keep them afloat. He suffered as the suffering of the poor continued unabated, and he had other sorrows. It is an indication of both his worries and his faith that between 9 October 1828, and 13 May 1832, he had caused no fewer than 2,773 Masses to be offered for the success of the establishment at Richmond Street, Dublin, which subsequently became famous as the O'Connell Schools.

One cause of deep sorrow occurred in 1827 when Brother Philip Halley of the Preston foundation called on the Protestant vicar and declared his intention of 'renouncing the errors of the Church of Rome'. It was Saturday, 14 April, and the vicar arranged a public recantation for the following day, Easter Sunday. Halley made his statement before an overflow congregation and was given a position as tutor in a local gentleman's house.

Edmund Rice was in Manchester when he heard of the recantation, and he would have gone to Preston had he not been dissuaded by the advice of Manchester clergy. Instead, he sent Brother Francis Phelan to meet and talk with Halley, but the mission was not a success – at least at the time. Towards the end of June, however, Halley returned to his monastery, renounced his recantation and signed a statement reaffirming his belief in the Catholic Church. Eventually, he arrived back in Mount Sion where, according to *The Waterford Mirror*, 'he gave evidence of sincere repentance'. What subsequently became of the unhappy former Brother is not known: his name disappeared from the records, but for a period he caused Edmund Rice the most acute distress.

There were more sorrows in 1832 when a cholera epidemic raged through most of Ireland. It made its appearance towards the end of March and existing hospitals soon became totally inadequate to cope. Edmund directed the Brothers to help in every possible way, and in Thurles and Dungarvan, monasteries and schools were vacated to make room for victims. The newly-built Sexton School was also made available in Limerick which 'was enveloped in a suffocating fog' on the night of 25 May. The first sufferers were struck down next day and the Brothers 'were all day long to be seen at the bedside of sufferers, attending to every call, soothing every pang, using every means possible to keep down the burning fever or to ease the agony of their tortured limbs. The night also found them at their posts, the silence of which was broken only by the cries of the patients calling aloud for the Brothers by their names, as their very presence seemed to have a soothing effect.'

In a letter to a Presentation nun, Edmund wrote: 'Our Limerick Brothers are attending the poor cholera patients. . . . They give a frightful account of the ravages it is making there, sixteen dead in their school one morning. . . . It is sticking to us here (in Dublin) but its malignity has much abated. An infidel or deist from this city ran away to Limerick in dread of it and there it catched (sic) him. He was brought into our Brothers' hospital where he made two confessions, being first instructed and assisted by one of our Brothers.' Edmund Rice always seemed to find something with which to console himself, and to him nothing could bring more consolation than the news of a soul set on the right road to salvation.

8

Support and Opposition

A Papal Brief was granted to the Institute of the Christian Brothers by Pope Pius VII in 1820; it was the first time that a society of lay religious Brothers in Ireland sought, or was given, such recognition, and it should have been an occasion of unreserved rejoicing. There was rejoicing, but there was also in the process, an extraordinary amount of controversy, and there was intrigue which was, in at least two instances, manifested in forged letters and spurious signatures. The story of the Brief is typical of many episodes in the life of Edmund Rice, with joy being clouded by sorrow, and with a determination to do what was right being dogged by trials and misrepresentation.

When Edmund founded his first monastery and school and attracted his first disciples, it was not his intention merely to provide for Waterford's poor children the education they so desperately needed. His vision was infinitely broader and his rationale was soundly practical. He wished for Papal approval because it would place the Congregation on the proper canonical footing, give a binding recognition to rules formulated to meet the peculiar needs of the Irish situation and, inevitably, give a status more likely to create a healthy influx of postulants.

Before he embarked on his apostolate, Edmund had written to and been encouraged by Pope Pius VI. Shortly after Mount Sion had been blessed in 1803, Bishop Hussey of Waterford had written to the Holy See that 'four holy men' there sought approbation of their rules, and early in 1804 Bishop John Power, Dr Hussey's successor, was telling Dr Francis Moylan, Bishop of Cork, that 'Mr Rice is pressing and begging to have application made to Rome for Bulls as the nuns have got.' This was a reference to a decree of approval for the Presentation nuns which was officially promulgated on 9 April 1805, and when Edmund Rice and his followers took their first annual vows in 1808, they were living according to the Presentation constitution with appropriate alterations and additions.

Bishop Power was advised by the Holy See that rules which the Institute would operate must be drawn up and 'only after the examination and approval of these rules can you hope to receive from the Sacred Congregation the desired Brief'. One question which caused a great deal of conflict concerned the nature of the Brief. Should it, like that granted to the French Order of the De La Salle Brothers by Pope Benedict XIII in 1724, place the Institute directly under the Holy See and under the control of a Superior General, or should it, like that accorded to the Presentation Sisters, place it under the authority of the local bishop? Edmund Rice favoured the former.

From the beginning, the Institute had its own special qualities of spirituality and outlook, and Edmund hoped that it would become a unified, closely-knit organisation, unswervingly loyal to its founding principles and having its particular stamp of commitment which would allow it to operate at maximum efficiency under a centralised governmental system. Under a system of diocesan control, Brothers in different dioceses would inevitably, in the course of time, develop traditions along individual lines and, while all might acknowledge a common founder, they would lack the benefit of having a common leader. On the most practical level, there would be the inescapable difficulty of bishops deploying available Brothers to the sectional, rather than the general, interest.

With houses being established in different dioceses, and with bishops of varying views and priorities coming and going, a society subject to the local ordinary could not realise Edmund Rice's purpose to the full spirit and letter, and could hardly be attuned to his visionary thinking. But the course he espoused, as he undoubtedly appreciated and would soon learn from unhappy experience, was fraught with hazards. There were bishops who were violently opposed to it, largely because they saw it as a threat to the exercise of their total diocesan control. A Congregation responsible to the Holy See and ruled by an independent Superior General would lead to a diminution of their authority, and in some instances, this attitude led to confrontations which were at best unpleasant and at worst bitter. Opposition took the extreme form of scandalous accusations made to Rome in forged letters.

Edmund Rice had some powerful allies as well as some discreditable enemies. His most influential friends included Archbishop John Troy of Dublin and his coadjutor, Dr Murray, both of whom became powerful champions. Other supporters in whose dioceses Institute houses were established included Archbishop Thomas Bray of Cashel and his coadjutor, Dr Patrick Everard, but determined opposition came from Bishop Robert Walsh, who succeeded Dr John Power in Waterford, and from the Bishop of Cork, Dr John Murphy.

In 1816 the constitution of the De La Salle Order was procured, and copies were sent to the eight houses of the Institute then in existence, with an exhortation that its provisions should be closely studied, and in August 1817, a meeting of Superiors was held at Mount Sion to discuss proposals relative to a set of rules suited to Irish conditions. The Brothers who assembled were not of one mind, for while the majority supported the idea of a Superior General, there were others who wished to give their allegiance to their bishop. They felt perhaps that under a Superior General their own authority as local Superiors would be diluted. In any event, a patient and painstaking process of finding the best way forward for the Institute was initiated, and when a formal application for a Brief was submitted, news of the move became generally known.

Dr Walsh, who had succeeded as Bishop of Waterford in 1817, was not only against the granting of a Brief on the De La Salle lines, but he had a noted antipathy to the Christian Brothers in general and to Edmund Rice in particular. He had his reasons and, as will be seen, they were discreditable ones, but it was especially unfortunate that a person of his very doubtful credentials should have been elevated to the Waterford See at this time, or indeed at all. The contrast in attitudes between him and his predecessor was nothing short of remarkable, and Dr Walsh lost no time in efforts to influence the Vatican against Edmund Rice when his views on the question of the Brief were requested by the Holy See.

In 1818 he wrote to the Cardinal Prefect of Propaganda: 'Indeed most of the bishops of Munster have written to me deprecating the conduct of some monks and protesting loudly of having a perpetual chief or general among them as they would wish to have by the introduction of the Bull of Benedict XIII relative to the Christian Schools of France (i.e. the De La Salle Order) into Ireland – this is what the bishops, priests and laity are not inclined to have done. My object is and it is necessary (whereas they are thus unruly and not disposed to live subject to pastoral and clerical superiors) . . . to order that they shall not receive the Sacraments. Without adhering to their original discipline nothing can go well. I hope y'll give no support to Rice's wishes or introducing the Bull of Benedictine XIII here.'

Dr Walsh's response was both dishonest and inaccurate and it was symptomatic of an orchestrated campaign which had got under way and which was aimed at sabotaging efforts to obtain the desired Brief. On 1 August 1818, an astonishing letter, allegedly signed by six Brothers, was sent to Rome. It stated: 'Hearing with great surprise that the business we thought lay at rest was privately agitated and not told unto us as well as to other members of the Institute in Ireland – to wit, of introducing the Bull of Benedict XIII relative to the Christian Schools of France by which they require the appointment of a perpetual general in the place of the superintendence of the bishops, we then, the undersigned monks of the houses of Dungarvan, Cork, Youghal, Clonmel, Carrick-on-Suir do solemnly protest against the innovation of introducing or appointing a Perpetual General in our institute which would withdraw us from under the protection and spiritual care of our bishops to whom we have promised obedience.' The letter added: 'Without being consulted about the appointing of the General, and only hearing report that it was the intention of some of the Superiors to have Mr. Rice appointed – had we been consulted we would object and protest against him as unfit and not capable of filling such a situation. And at present we protest in the most solemn manner against such an act fraudulently and subreptiously (sic) attempted.'

This letter was not merely a blatant forgery, but also a stupid one. Houses in Clonmel and Youghal were not even in existence at the time, and of the six names appended, there are no records that four ever belonged to the Institute. More than a century later, a handwriting expert, Mr Arthur C. Brooks of Naas, Co. Kildare, was provided with all the necessary evidence and samples of authentic handwriting, and his specialist opinion was that the letter had been written by a Father Patrick O'Meagher, parish priest of Dungarvan. But the campaign reached a new level of malice when, in September 1818, a lengthy document was sent to the Cardinal Prefect of Propaganda, allegedly bearing the signatures of seventeen parish priests of the Waterford diocese: 'It may not be amiss', it went in part, 'to give Your Eminence a brief outline of Rice the Monk's life, in order to form an opinion of his now malicious interference – this man sometime was a dealer in cattle and common butcher in the streets of Waterford. Your Eminence will judge from this, his slaughtering profession, of the savageness of his nature and absence of tender sensibility and want of human feeling. This impertinent intruder in the affairs of the sanctuary was of habits irregular and of desires lustful. . . . This is a truth we all know and so do the laity of Waterford. . . . It is even known to some now living in the city of Rome – ashamed of his misfortunes, he entered on a religious life and how happy the change, if he be truly repented and did not meddle in other people's concerns. Not still satisfied, this wretched man's ambition also is to become a perpetual general of his Institute in order to lord it over the priests and bishops, to be under no controal (sic) by the introduction of Benedict the 13th's Bull into Ireland which we humbly protest against for piety sake.'

Names and locations of seventeen priests were listed, and the letter ended with the addendum: 'Finding we had not space or time to send this document to the other pastors of the diocese, whose approbation and direction we had to send forward their names to Your Eminence, and also that of professors of the Seminary at Waterford, with three deservitars of parishes and fifty coadjutors besides: we hope the above signatures will be full sufficient to attest and satisfy

Yr. Eminence as to the veracity and sincerity of this remonstrance.'

As in the case of the letter alleged to have come from six Brothers, this document was also subsequently proved to be a forgery by Padre Girolamo Moretti, the greatest handwriting expert in the Italy of his time – a view later confirmed by investigations carried out by the firm of Charles A. Aspel, Jr., Washington D.C. But the document did not deceive the Cardinal Prefect: in a letter to Archbishop Troy he referred to 'witnesses of whom we have not the slightest knowledge, many in the same hand, many repeated several times, others illegible'. As a result, Dr Troy was directed to have an Apostolic Notary appointed in each diocese to certify all documents forwarded to the Sacred Congregation. When Edmund Rice was made aware of these remarkable efforts to discredit him and prevent the granting of a Brief, he must have been perplexed and pained. He was not, however, deterred. As was his custom, he sought strength and solace through prayer, he went for advice to friends whose wisdom and prudence were known to him, and he consulted with his Brother Superiors. Work proceeded on the preparation of a constitution based to a large extent on the De La Salle rules but with amendments geared to Irish conditions.

The final draft was submitted to Rome in 1819, and to it Archbishop Troy added a telling testimony: 'I certify that the Society of laics which supplicate the Holy See for approbation of their Institute, by means of their labour in promoting religion and the moral education of poor boys have done the greatest good for Religion not only in Dublin but also in other parts of this Kingdom. Furthermore, I testify that the aforesaid rules of this Society are adapted to the conditions of this country and very suitable for the propagation of the Institute. The testimony of other bishops in Ireland agrees with me in this matter.'

The Prefect of the Sacred Congregation, Cardinal Fontana, was doubtless delighted to receive Edmund Rice's application and to learn of the progress of the Institute. The previous year he had sent an open letter to the Irish hierarchy in which he spoke of the Bible schools established in almost every part of

Ireland in which 'under the pretence of charity, the inexperienced of both sexes, but particularly peasants and the poor, are allured by the blandishments, and even gifts, of the masters and infected with the fatal poison of depraved doctrines'. He exhorted the bishops to guard their flocks 'with diligence and with all discretion from these persons who are in the habit of thrusting themselves insidiously into the fold of Christ in order thereby to lead many unwary sheep astray'. The letter added: 'Do you labour with all your might to keep the orthodox youth from being corrupted by them, an object which will, I hope, be easily effected by the establishment of Catholic schools.'

Edmund Rice's apostolate was precisely the type of activity Cardinal Fontana was urging, and when the rules relating to the application for a Brief were submitted with Archbishop Troy's recommendation, he was obviously influential in pressing for an early conclusion. The rules were marginally altered and the final draft of the Brief was drawn up. It was signed by Pope Pius VII on 5 September 1820, and the news was conveyed to the Dublin coadjutor, Dr Murray. He informed Edmund Rice and wrote: 'I cannot tell you how much pleasure it gives me to find that your Institute has at length obtained the approbation of His Holiness. . . . God grant stability to an Institute that promises so fairly to be of essential benefit to the interests of religion in this country.'

The Brief was eventually delivered to Edmund Rice in January 1821, and established the first congregation of lay religious men in Ireland. It came less than twenty years after the first school had been set up, and the fact that it arrived with such speed despite the campaign against it showed the extent of the success achieved by Edmund and his followers and the reputation they enjoyed. But the arrival of the Brief did not mean that everything in the future would be plain sailing. Controversy would continue and some members of the Institute would, for sincere, conscientious reasons, decline to accept its terms and remain under the jurisdiction of their bishops.

A copy of the Brief was sent to every Brother and a meeting of those who had taken perpetual vows was arranged for Thurles in August 1821. Nineteen attended, and three others wrote excusing themselves but stating they would accept the majority decision. Discussions took place over a period of two days, and it was decided that a meeting would be held early the next year at Mount Sion to enable those willing to pronounce vows according to the new constitution. The first General Chapter would also be held, and a Superior General elected.

It is significant that no Brother from Cork was present at the Thurles meeting. The bishop, Dr Murphy, was intractably opposed to all non-diocesan institutions, irrespective of how rich a contribution they might make to the quality of life. The Cork Brothers were imbued with the soaring charity of their founder: they visited the male section of the city jail on Sundays and holy days, and the reputation of the North Monastery as an educational centre stood extremely high.

Richard Lovell Edgeworth, brother of the writer Maria, wrote of the North Monastery in 1824: "There is so much to say and approve of in this establishment that I really do not know where to begin. I was first struck by the appearance of discipline and obedience which seemed to pervade the whole. The countenances were in general cheerful, and though many were in indifferent clothing, yet the faces and hands were cleaner than in most schools of the same sort. I make no doubt but that the acquirements are equal to what might be expected from the unwearying zeal and constant attention of the disinterested instructors of this unique establishment.'

Bishop Murphy was clearly more interested in maintaining his authority than in helping and encouraging the type of development so warmly described by Edgeworth. He tried to get permanent control of the establishment by seeking to have a legal title to the property made out in his name and in 1825 requested the Superior to prove the Brothers' title.

His preoccupation with preserving an overlordship was also seen in relation to others. He had no objection to the presence of the Sisters of Charity, but he had a deep-rooted aversion to having in his diocese any nuns governed from Dublin. Stanhope Street, the Sisters' Generalate, was to him the 'headquarters of a foreign government' and his attitude so worried the Sisters' Superior General, Mother Mary Aikenhead, that she feared he would induce some of the nuns to break away from the parent organisation and set up a society under his control.

Things became so threatening that at the request of Mother Mary, Dr Murray of Dublin appealed to the Sacred Congregation, which took the unusual step of issuing a decree that 'Sisters who had already joined and those who would join in the future could not pass to any other religious order or institute without the special permission of the Holy See.' It is plain that Bishop Murphy looked on the Papal Brief with unbounded distaste, and he used every means available to him to dissuade the Cork Brothers from accepting its terms. While none of them attended the Thurles meeting, a number subsequently went to Mount Sion and, before returning to Cork, made their vows in accordance with the Papally approved rules. Edmund Rice, his business sense as practical as ever, sent a Brother with £400 to the French home of Sir George Gould, the landlord of the North Monastery property, and secured the freehold for the Institute. With the complete backing of Papal authority, the Cork Brothers were independent of a meddlesome bishop.

Dr Murphy appealed successfully to one member of the Institute who had not yet accepted the Brief, Brother Michael Austin Riordan. An architect and a man of noted piety and talent, he had distinguished himself in the North Monastery and, at Dr Murphy's urging, he took up residence in a building which had been vacated by the Presentation nuns at Douglas Street. He opened a temporary school in Cat Lane off Barrack Street in July, 1827, and was soon joined by two postulants. The Congregation which emerged came to be known and celebrated in the educational scene as the Presentation Brothers and in later years it also sought and obtained a Papal Brief.

Over subsequent years the Presentation Brothers expanded their teaching apostolate to many parts of Ireland, and distinguished themselves both in their service to education and their service to the poor. That they eventually sought a Papal Brief may be seen as an endorsement of the wisdom, foresight and logicality shown by Edmund Rice in his approach but, more importantly, the Presentation Congregation was inspired by Edmund's extraordinary charisma, imbued with his spiritual vision and motivated by his practical compassion. As much as the Christian Brothers, the Presentation Brothers regard him as their founder, and it is a matter of some interest that before the Brief of Pope Pius VII was granted, Edmund and his followers were sometimes called Presentation monks because, to a large degree, they were guided by the rule governing the Presentation Sisters.

The unhappy relationship between Brothers and bishop in Cork was the sort of situation Edmund would have found very distressing. It was not of his making, however, and he would not allow it to hamper the work to which he had dedicated himself and his Institute. The unpleasant experience demonstrated effectively the wisdom of and the need for a Brief placing the Institute under the control of a Superior General and responsible to the Holy See. To operate efficiently, it was essential that Brothers could be sent from place to place to found, supervise or work in foundations, and this would be impossible were bishops like Dr Murphy to determine where the Brothers went and what they did.

The Papal Brief was formally accepted at Mount Sion on 20 January 1822, the Feast of the Holy Name of Jesus. Nineteen Brothers had completed an eight day retreat conducted by Father Peter Kenney, S.J., and the Brief was read aloud following the recitation of the Veni Creator. The Superiors who were present then formed the first General Chapter and Brother Edmund Ignatius Rice was chosen the first Superior General.

9

Scandal in Waterford

It has been noted that Edmund Rice showed a life-long reticence concerning his private thoughts and affairs. He left no personal memoirs and he did not keep a spiritual diary. But he did leave some insights in the letters he wrote, and these are of primary importance in piecing together a fully rounded portrait of the man. From this portrait one outstanding and incontrovertible quality emerges: his faith in and devotion to the Catholic Church was total. Everything he did related to this faith and devotion, and if his apostolate of bringing education to poor boys succeeded only in equipping them to enter with distinction into diverse areas of employment, he would not have been satisfied. He wanted them, above all, to be good Catholics with a high sense of morality in its widest sense, and with attitudes which were deeply God-oriented.

A particularly revealing insight can be seen in a letter he wrote in 1810 to his friend, Mr Bryan Bolger, an architect and surveyor, concerning a business matter in which they were involved. 'I am sorry to be giving you so much trouble', the letter stated, 'perhaps it may come my way to do as much for you; however, I hope God will supply our inability in this way; it's a poor thing, I must own, to be expecting the reward of labour from creatures who frequently are forgetful and ungrateful for favours done them, but let us do ever so little for God, we will be sure He will never forget it, nor let it pass unrewarded. How many of our actions are lost for want of applying them to this end, and were we to know the merit and value of only going from one street to another to serve a neighbour for the love of God, we should prize it more than Gold or Silver. . . . One thing you may be sure of, that whilst you work for God, whether you succeed or not, He will amply reward you.'

This approach of doing everything for the service and love of God was the corner-stone of life as he lived it. 'The world and everything in it is continually changing', he wrote to a Presentation nun, 'which proves to us that there is nothing permanent under the Sun, and that perfect happiness is not to be expected but in another world.' To Brother John Austin Grace on his appointment as Superior of the Preston foundation, he offered advice: 'You being yet very young in religion, and placed over a senior Brother, will require great watchfulness over yourself to perform well the task which is assigned to you, and you should beg frequently of God light and Grace to effect it, and above all, beg Him to give you the virtue of humility which is so necessary for religious in every station, but particularly for those who have the care or direction of others. If only you acquire this virtue, it will always guide you safely let your paths be ever so cross or difficult. Never allow vain notions of your own sense, abilities or other natural or acquired qualifications to take root in your mind, but always beseech God to make known to you your sins and imperfections.'

These brief extracts give an indication of Edmund Rice's own spirituality, and of the spiritual values he wished to inculcate in his Institute. As an extension of his commitment, he concerned himself wherever he saw the interests of Catholicism threatened. One controversial issue which disturbed him was a proposal that a Royal veto should operate in relation to the appointment of bishops. It was first mooted in 1808 by the liberal-minded politician, Henry Grattan, and his allies at Westminster, and its purpose was to conciliate opposition to support for the national seminary, St Patrick's College, Maynooth, which was aided by an annual parliamentary grant. Demands for Catholic emancipation were growing, and Grattan felt that the resistance of his fellow Protestants would be softened if the English government were to have control over episcopal appointments in Ireland. A Rescript from Rome in 1814 gave permission for a limited amount of control, to general dismay in Ireland.

The Irish hierarchy rejected the Rescript, and in this

reflected the views of the vast majority of the laity, although most of the Catholic English and the Vicars Apostolic were prepared to accept it. Edmund Rice was in no doubt about the danger of political interference in the affairs of the Church, and in a letter to the Jesuit priest, Father Peter Kenney, he wrote: 'We are all in confusion on account of this Roman Rescript on the veto. If His Holiness should concur in what has been done, that respect which has always been paid by the Irish will suffer very materially. It is considered here that the treatment was most contemptible to the Irish bishops, clergy and people. May the Almighty preserve us from Schism and every other mischief with which we are threatened by this wicked veto.'

As it happened, the veto was shelved because of the strength of the Irish opposition, and the danger of schism disappeared, but nearer to Edmund Rice's own doorstep a situation arose within the Church itself which was a cause of much dissention and considerable scandal, and which necessitated decisive intervention by the Holy See. It came about following the death of Dr John Power, Bishop of Waterford and Lismore, who had been a friend of Edmund's and a wholehearted supporter of his Institute. The death was in itself a matter of deep personal sorrow for Edmund Rice, but the consequences were painful in the extreme. They had widespread ramifications on the local scene, and throughout the Province of Munster, and at a time when Edmund Rice was seeking a Papal Brief, there was an overspill of remarkable vilification to the Vatican concerning him and his Institute.

Dr Power had been a strong advocate of obtaining a Brief and had secured the backing of Bishop Moylan of Cork, who died in 1815. The deaths of the two prelates robbed Edmund Rice of influential champions because, as we have seen, the new Bishop of Cork, Dr Murphy, was an intransigent diocesan man who was altogether opposed to the terms of the Brief, but Dr Robert Walsh, who succeeded the Waterford See, posed different and more serious problems. He was not only hostile to a Brief but also to Edmund Rice and the Christian Brothers as a whole. On a more fundamental level, his administration led to a corruption of the values which Edmund held sacred.

The four-year period which followed the death of Bishop Power in January 1816, covers a singularly dark chapter in the history of the Waterford diocese, and there is ample evidence that standards among a small section of the clergy were at a very low ebb. There was trouble from the time the succession process got under way: at a meeting of diocesan clergy in Carrick-on-Suir, Father Thomas Flannery, parish priest of Clonmel, was proposed, but his nomination did not find favour with the Munster hierarchy or with many of his fellow-priests because of the serious weaknesses of character which they imputed to him. Fr Flannery was requested to step down, and did so only when the Bishop of Kerry, Dr Charles Sughrue, threatened him with public exposure and disgrace.

At another meeting in Carrick-on-Suir on 8 April 1816 Fr Robert Walsh, parish priest of Dungarvan and a friend of Fr Flannery's was named, but not before twenty-four priests had withdrawn in protest against the manner in which proceedings were conducted. His nomination was also rejected by the bishops, and one priest wrote to Rome asking that the entire management of the appointment be placed in the hands of the Munster hierarchy, 'as they are the only persons who can give that information which will enable the Holy See to make a decision advantageous to the peace and religion of the diocese'. This letter, which was signed by thirty priests, charged that Fr Walsh's nomination was uncanonical and that the man himself was 'totally unfit to govern' the diocese. The bishops meanwhile had put forward the name of Dr B. Crotty, President of Maynooth, but a campaign against him was mounted by Fr Walsh's supporters because he did not belong to the diocese and they did not want 'a foreign prelate' forced on them.

Eventually, Rome astonishingly disregarded the bishops' advice, and appointed Fr Walsh. He was consecrated in August 1817, after an interregnum of eighteen months and, aware of a potentially dangerous development, the Munster hierarchy took the unusual step of extracting a promise from him that he would not appoint Fr Patrick O'Meagher as his successor in Dungarvan. There were clear signs of trouble to come when, despite his pledge, one of the new bishop's first acts was to place Fr O'Meagher in charge of Dungarvan parish. Charges had been made that Bishop Walsh and Fr O'Meagher had been in collusion concerning simoniacal practices.

According to Fr William Howley, parish priest of Clerihan, Clonmel, 'the clergy was divided into scandalous factions' over the succession question, and the appointment of Dr Walsh was influenced 'by the factious clergy through their fraudulent intrigues to the Holy See in spite of the more responsible bishops of the Province, and even of the nation'. In his *Parochial History of Waterford and Lismore*, Patrick Canon Power wrote that Bishop Walsh 'though of personal integrity and excellence seems, unfortunately for himself and the diocese, to have rather lacked clearness of view, judgement of character and that firmness of purpose which in a crisis is so necessary for a bishop. . . . Certain it was that during the closing years of his episcopacy, there was much unrest in the diocese. . . . The source and fountainhead of the trouble was the poor bishop's patronage for a certain parish priest who had gained his confidence and basely abused it to the detriment of Dr Walsh and the peace of the diocese.'

Canon Power was patently more charitable than factual in his summation of Bishop Walsh, for while Fr O'Meagher was the primary cause of scandal and debasement of moral values, the bishop showed little integrity or excellence in continuing his support for a priest whose unworthiness was beyond question: in his vindictive treatment of priests who had opposed his appointment, and in the slanderous and blatantly false accusations he made to Rome in respect of Edmund Rice and others.

Edmund was close to some of the priests who had taken a stand against Bishop Walsh's appointment, especially Fr Pierce Power, who was his parish priest and chaplain to the Mount Sion community, and while there is no record that he became embroiled in the acrimonious succession controversy, a letter of March 1816, suggests that he was involved – or at least charged with being so. The letter, written by Dr Kieran Marum, Bishop of Ossory, to Brother Austin Dunphy went, in part: 'I beg to state that in my opinion the interference ascribed to Mr Rice could be warranted only by very extraordinary circumstances. May God preserve the church of

Waterford from those evils which the unhappy division to which you allude may very naturally lead to. Religion may suffer irreparably, charity may perish in the conflict and the worst and most destructive spirit that hell could send forth, a spirit of party, may distract and desolate the diocese.' Whatever the precise nature of 'the interference ascribed to Mr Rice', it is certain that Dr Walsh knew he was among the considerable body of bishops, clergy and laity who did not favour him, and he would make his feelings known in no uncertain terms.

Through the Christian Brothers and the Presentation Sisters in Dungarvan, Edmund was kept well informed of what was happening there. And events justified only too fully his earlier misgivings. The situation deteriorated to the extent that a Synod of Munster bishops was held in Fermoy on 18 November 1818, to hear charges of immoral conduct on the part of Fr O'Meagher, as well as various accusations against the bishop relating to his personal conduct, the administration of the diocese and the victimisation of priests who had opposed him.

No decisive action was taken by the Synod, which was content to accept a promise from Dr Walsh that changes for the better would be made, but in the event things worsened, and in July 1819, some Waterford clergy 'seeing that the evil was proceeding too far and threatening the ruin of religion', requested Dr Walsh to investigate charges against Fr O'Meagher and to 'adopt such measures as would put an end to the scandals that are spreading'. The investigation took place in the Presentation convent, Dungarvan, at which many witnesses deposed on oath serious moral charges against Fr O'Meagher. Fr O'Meagher was, however, exonerated and the verdict was announced at all Masses in Dungarvan and district the following Sunday.

The investigation was carried out over a number of days by a tribunal composed of Dr Walsh and about ten priests, a number of whom withdrew in protest against the way in which it was being conducted. They drew up a document announcing that they would appeal to the Archbishop of Cashel. It was handed to Brother James Joseph Mulcahy, Superior of the Christian Brothers' School in Dungarvan, for delivery to Dr Walsh. In a sworn statement Brother Mulcahy subsequently told of a plot arranged by Fr O'Meagher and his adherents 'for the purpose of destroying the character of the nuns of Dungarvan'. It was like something out of horror fiction, and when Brother Mulcahy informed the nuns about it 'they were obliged to employ armed men at night for a considerable time both inside and outside their garden'.

As this incredible state of affairs continued, Rome was bombarded from both sides by letters, memorials, protests, charges, counter-charges and pleas for intervention. Bishop William Coppinger, of the diocese of Cloyne and Ross, wrote asking for 'definite action and the most inflexible rigidity', and a remonstrance which he drafted was sent to Edmund Rice, who secured the signatures of sixty-four of Waterford's most prominent citizens. It was also intended as an appeal to the Holy See concerning 'the lamentable scandals that have arisen', and a similar memorial was forwarded to Rome by the laity in Carrick-on-Suir. The Sacred Congregation was faced with a mounting pile of contradictory documents and, with a touch of desperation, it appealed to the Archbishop of Cashel for guidance.

Having listed some of the charges made against Dr Walsh, it stated that 'the bishop himself has told us that all is grand except for a few turbulent priests'. It mentioned an accusation that Dr Walsh 'constantly persecuted the Presentation nuns and the Directors of the Christian Schools' and pleaded: 'For God's sake, let us have the truth and quickly.'

Eventually the Munster bishops took decisive action. At a meeting in Fermoy on 13 June 1820, they recommended that Dr Walsh should be suspended and an administrator appointed. In his submissions to the Holy See, Dr Walsh displayed a striking talent for colourful invective. Dr Coppinger he described as 'an old, wild, strange man who (because of the wildness of his manner and his imbecility, the undersigned believes mental), has for years past prejudiced the cause of Catholics in Ireland as well as England', and he later added: 'Your Eminence will perceive the necessity of reducing to silence this old bishop, or of sitting on him, as probably he will never desist from involving the government of Rome and the Catholics and all in inextricable troubles.'

In a similar vein he castigated Edmund Rice as 'once a butcher who is the leader of the discontented against episcopal authority. . . . The above-named Rice is a brother of a good-for-nothing Religious of the Order of St Augustine . . . a turbulent layman, once a common butcher on the stalls and a public fornicator.' He also rounded on the Christian Brothers, alleging that 'much criticism and public scandal have very often been the consequence of the liberty they have of going to the Fairs, and to the Markets, buying and selling cattle and collecting Rents and executing seizures, like common landlords, against the poor to exact the Rent'. This was a ludicrous charge and obviously referred to Dungarvan and Cappoquin, where the Brothers depended for their maintenance on the management of a farm, but apart from Bishop Walsh there is no suggestion that they engaged in seizures or exactions against the poor.

Verifiable facts were not a strong point with Dr Walsh. Most likely influenced by Father O'Meagher, he did everything in his power to discredit the Brothers in the eyes of the Holy See, and to prevent their Institute from getting a Brief. In another letter he wrote that 'from the general tenor of their conduct and Rice's, on whose intermeddling spirit I mean not to dwell, who did much mischief among the clergy here by the diffusion of uncharitableness all over the country during the interregnum, I must declare that there is much to censure on the part of these Monks that I avow to my certain knowledge'. He talked of the Brothers as 'quarrelling among each other – ejecting each other from their houses – rambling about as they will without the leave of either bishop, pastor or director'.

The Holy See was not impressed by Dr Walsh's unsupported accusations which were, to a large part if not wholly, inspired by Father O'Meagher, who showed an unbridled enmity towards Edmund Rice and the Christian Brothers because they were not indifferent to his conduct in Dungarvan, and he went to astonishing extremes to slander them and sabotage their application for a Brief. The letter referred to in a previous chapter which was alleged to have been signed by seventeen Waterford priests was later proved by hand-writing experts to have been a forgery by Father

O'Meagher, and it gives an indication of the man who enjoyed the continuing support and friendship of Dr Walsh.

The letter was written in September 1818, and was primarily intended as a refutation of charges made against Bishop Walsh. It referred to the memorial signed by sixty-four Waterford laymen as having been organised 'through a monk by the name of Rice and a silly, crack-brained curate of the name of John Sheehan', and went on to give a colourful distortion of Rice the Monk's life. It was a puerile exercise in vituperation and was, not surprisingly, ignored.

The Holy See might, perhaps, have taken more heed of less intemperate language: as it happened, Father O'Meagher was suspended and is reported to have shown 'evidence of sincere repentance'. He was given a pension and lived in Dungarvan until his death in 1834. Dr Walsh was summoned to Rome, but because of the serious state of his health, he was not deposed. He retired to the Roman suburb of Tivoli, and resided there until he died in 1821. A period of deep unrest and great unhappiness in the Waterford diocese came to an end and the general relief was shared by Edmund Rice. The purging process was fully vindicated and his reputation, and that of the Brothers, remained untarnished.

Two interior views of Edmund Rice's house (*J. T. Dunne*)

St Patrick's Penal Church, Waterford (*J. T. Dunne*)

Edmund Rice's personal Bible (*J. T. Dunne*)

10

Pay-school Conflict

The Papal Brief granted by Pope Pius VII in 1821 established the Institute of the Christian Brothers as the first ever congregation of male religious in Ireland, and Edmund Rice was chosen Superior General at the first General Chapter, with Brothers Patrick Ellis and Austin Dunphy the two Assistants provided for in the terms of the Brief. The issue of the Papal document was a cause of gratitude, joy and celebration; nevertheless one of its clauses was looked on with reservation, and it is an indication of Edmund Rice's determined character that he took immediate steps to seek an alteration. The clause was Article 5, which stated that the Brothers 'shall teach the children gratis, never accepting anything as a reward or retribution either from them or their parents'. This was considered too restrictive and, following Edmund's lead, the General Chapter requested a change; it asked for permission to open pay-schools.

There were excellent reasons, and they were listed in an appeal to Rome: 'Witnessing in many instances the deplorable state of the children of Roman Catholics in easy and comfortable circumstances of life, exposed to so many dangers from a want of religious instruction (several of them going to Protestant schools), the Brothers entertain strong desires of extending the advantages of religious education to this class of person by opening pay-schools for their reception and employing the emoluments arising from them to further extension of the instruction of the poor.'

Edmund Rice was immensely practical. He also tended to be pragmatic wherever the interests of the very poor and their spiritual welfare were concerned. From personal experience he was only too well aware of what the situation was. On the one hand, there were many thousands of children whose parents were in such a state of destitution that they could not afford to pay even a halfpenny a week, and these were his primary concern.

In setting up schools for them, the most daunting obstacles had to be overcome. Money was the main problem, and in more than one instance Brothers whose function it was to teach were forced to spend hours begging from door to door so that the schools could remain open. In a letter written from Limerick, Brother Austin Dunphy put the scene in perspective when he wrote: 'We find from experience how galling it is when, after spending five days in weighty schools, we must sally out on the sixth day to beg from house to house for pennies and halfpennies to support us for the ensuing week. With all our dunning and exertions we find the collections diminishing fast. . . .' Apart from begging, one of the other main sources of income was annual charity sermons, but because of antipathy on the part of a bishop or a local parish priest, the sermons were occasionally prohibited.

On the other hand, there were parents who could contribute something, however modest, to the education of their children, and Edmund Rice considered that pay-schools for this category would serve a number of admirable purposes. In the first place, they would provide spiritually-oriented instruction for the better-off and, in the second, they would produce revenue which would ensure the survival of existing free institutions and the setting up of others. They would also inevitably lead to more vocations to the priesthood and the brotherhood. It might appear that the wisdom, the basic commonsense of Edmund's attitude in this regard would find unaminous endorsement and encouragement: on the contrary, the pay-school issue was to become a cause of acrimony and bitter controversy. It would come close to causing the Institute irreparable damage as conflicting views clashed, personal enmities grew and factions tended to become entrenched on the opposite sides of a widening breach.

The first request for leave to open a pay-school was made in January 1823, and the Holy See referred it to Dr Patrick Kelly who had succeeded Dr Robert Walsh as Bishop of Waterford in 1822. Dr Kelly was one of a number of bishops who did not show the capacity to appreciate fully the splendour of the Rice vision and who were not prepared to give unqualified backing to the dedicated work it demanded. Born in Kilkenny, he studied in Lisbon and after serving as President of Birchfield College, Kilkenny, was appointed Bishop of Richmond, Virginia, U.S.A., in 1820. Two years later he was translated to Waterford where he remained until his death in 1829. He had, according to W. J. Fitzgerald in his *Life and Times of Dr Doyle (JKL)** the heart of a true patriot, but 'his demeanour was haughty and from the first his appointment may be said to have been unpopular. He was determined, dogmatical and self-willed. . . . As a churchman he was rigid, occasionally illiberal, sometime despotic. Erudite, ascetic and talented, but without much profundity of judgment, he was not infrequently viewed with feelings of awe. . . .'

One incident which occurred shortly after his arrival shows that Dr Kelly's later severe and unjustified treatment of Edmund Rice was not an isolated case. The Augustinians of Dungarvan had requested, and obtained, from Dr Robert Walsh permission to erect a new church, but the friars did not seek confirming permission from Dr Kelly on his accession. Because of this rather trivial oversight, the new bishop ordered the church closed, and had an interdict placed on its door. The Holy See, which already had had sufficient trouble with the Waterford diocese to last a lifetime, was forced eventually to intervene. It decreed that the church be reopened, but as a sop to Dr Kelly's pride, the Augustinians were requested to apologise to the prelate, and they were not allowed to hold church-door collections for two years, although one annual collection within the church was permitted.

When the Holy See first sought Dr Kelly's views on the pay-school question, he replied that there was 'no lack of Catholic schools in my diocese, even for the rich', but he added: 'That is not to say that the petition of the Brothers should not be looked on with favour. The increase in the number of Catholic schools is not a bad thing, neither would the new schools about which the request is made greatly interfere with schools already established for the poor. It is also possible that some

*JKL were the initials used by Bishop James Doyle of Kildare and Leighlin (1786–1834).

financial aid might thus be obtained for the maintenance of the Brother Monks.' While the bishop did not show an overwhelming enthusiasm for pay-schools, he did not reject the idea. A remarkable and inexplicable change of attitude on Dr Kelly's part was, however, soon to become apparent.

When Edmund Rice received no decision in response to the petition of January 1823, he renewed his application in 1824. By then he had completed a visit as Superior General to the Institute's foundations, and his first-hand knowledge of the situation was enhanced. He repeated his arguments and pointed out that while the British Parliament had, in that year, allocated £32,000 to Bible School Societies 'for the purpose of diffusing their principles among the poor of this Kingdom', the Brothers had practically no income to support them in their work. He obviously felt that Vatican reluctance to accede to his request sprang from a fear that the poor might suffer as a result, and pledged that should a majority of the Irish Hierarchy at any future time decide that the poor were being neglected as a consequence of pay-schools, the Brothers would cease to accept payments.

The renewed petition was, like the original, referred to Dr Kelly, and for reasons which are very obscure, he wrote an astonishingly damning and inaccurate letter in reply. The bishop was still a relatively inexperienced prelate and was, perhaps, not completely informed about either the educational position in his diocese or the effectiveness of the Brothers' educational methods. There is also the distinct possibility that he had sought the advice of clerics who opposed Edmund Rice in the affairs concerning Bishop Walsh and Father O'Meagher. In any event, his response was startlingly different from the neutral opinion he had expressed less than a year earlier: 'I am decidedly of the opinion that the petition should not be granted', he wrote. 'I see no reason for such an application, especially as it does not seem right in this wretched country, in which tailors and cobblers, and even women, assume at will the right to interpret Sacred Scripture and to found new religious societies, to entrust religious instruction with any solemnity to laics, even though they be Monks, and that what has been done here should not perhaps have been done. . . . Catholic schools abound in the South of

Ireland and no Catholic child attends a Protestant school for the want of a Catholic school, though they may attend them for other reasons. These are, however, few here because our Catholics abhor not only the houses and schools of the heretics, but even their very name. And even if in my diocese, though it is not true, there was any want of Catholic schools in which the well-to-do Catholics could be educated, the aforesaid Monks could not provide a remedy because of their illiteracy.'

Dr Kelly's letter was equally lacking in truth and charity. It was inaccurate, superficial and slanderous, and the suggestion that Papal approval should not have been given to the Institute (his mention of 'even women' was, apparently, an oblique reference to the Presentation Sisters and other orders of nuns) was a ludicrous denial of the vast amount of good already achieved. At the time the bishop was writing, there were thirty-eight Catholic pay-schools in Waterford city, but most of them were described as 'miserable garretts' or 'wretched lodgings' and in the majority of cases, the standard of instruction and the level of accommodation did not justify the fees charged. A total of 107 Catholic pupils were in fact, attending one or other of the city's thirty-two Protestant schools.

The reference by Dr Kelly to illiteracy is incomprehensible. There was ample evidence regarding the dramatic results the Brothers' teaching methods had achieved. The accusation of illiteracy is clearly ridiculous when applied to Edmund Rice himself; to Austin Dunphy, a most able writer and manager; to Patrick Ellis, who had been professor of mathematics in the Waterford diocesan college before he joined the Institute; to Patrick Murphy, a well-educated member of a wealthy local family; to James Dollard, a native of Dublin who had been a highly successful businessman; to Roger Ryan who was proficient in Latin and Greek in Dublin. All were mature of age and their educational programme embraced grammar, geography, mensuration, navigation, surveying and book-keeping in addition to the three *R*s. How Bishop Kelly could, in conscience, use the term 'illiteracy' of such men is altogether mysterious, but he did. In doing so, and in questioning the wisdom of granting a Brief, he was adding to the perplexing number of unwarranted difficulties thrown in the way of the Institute's smooth progress.

Edmund Rice was subjected to an almost unending series of trials, tribulations, rebuffs and hurts in the course of his apostolate. Bishops, priests, his own colleagues and anonymous troublemakers were involved, but he accepted every cross that came his way willingly and without recrimination. Towards the end of 1824, he and his assistants wrote to the Sacred Congregation defending the Institute against imputations that they were 'teaching false doctrine to the poor children in their schools'. The charges were made by an unidentified person who added 'that instead of being a benefit, it were much better that their Society had never been instituted and that they did not deserve in any manner the support or protection of Rome'.

The replying letter, addressed to Pope Leo XII, shows a mixture of bewilderment, sincerity and grit. It pointed out that the religious instruction given was based on a catechism approved by the four Irish archbishops, and it expressed surprise that the unknown accuser 'never once admonished the party who taught such (false) doctrine'. It added: 'Your memorialists, not wishing to have such imputations remain against them on the records of the Sacred Congregation, most humbly beg that Your Holiness may give them an opportunity of proving their innocence by giving directions to have the person making this charge called upon to explain to your memorialists the nature of it, and state by whom, to whom and in what place this false doctrine has been taught, and should it turn out that through inadvertence or want of explanation, colour may be given to found such charge, your memorialists pledge themselves that they will, with all humility and docility, receive and adopt such explanations as will be in strict conformity with the doctrine of the Church. In making this request of your Holiness, your memorialists do not mean to insinuate a wish to have the name of the person who has made this charge known to them, unless it is found absolutely necessary for acquitting themselves; the only thing they require is the giving them an opportunity of justifying themselves or of correcting their errors (if they have fallen into any) and thereby have this charge which has caused them so much pain taken off the records of the Sacred Congregation, and if this can be done without having the name of the person brought forth, the wish of your memorialists is, that it may for ever remain in oblivion.'

Nothing more was heard of the anonymous accusations, and while the petitions of 1823 and 1824 were not granted, Edmund Rice remained convinced of the benefits of pay-schools. The issue went into abeyance for a number of years, and when it came to the forefront again, it became clear that a considerable number of the Brothers opposed the idea because they were sincerely of the opinion that the Institute had one exclusive purpose, and that was the gratuitous instruction of the poor. They argued that to accept money would be contrary to the letter of the Papal Brief and to the spirit of the Institute, and some feared that the best teachers would be assigned to the pay-schools and that the poor, for one reason or another, would suffer as a result.

Prior to the General Chapter of 1838 at which Edmund Rice resigned as Superior General, he wrote a circular letter to members in which he set out his thinking with lucidity and clarity. He wrote of 'the depressed state of some of our houses and the impossibility of supporting others without the painful, dissipating and dangerous alternative of perpetual begging even against the wish, or rather at the unpleasant expense of incurring the displeasure, of priests and even bishops also, the injurious effect of (sic) such a system must have on the schools, by having some of the best conductors absent from them on this begging mission'. These and other considerations, he went on, 'lead me and other Brothers to the conclusion that there is but one alternative left for the support of some of our houses already established, and the further propagation of our Institute on a permanent and independent footing in Ireland; that is the gradual establishment of pay-schools for the education of the children of shopkeepers and decent tradesmen, a class who scarcely ever receive a religious education, the proceeds of such schools would enable the Brothers to educate the poor in greater numbers.'

At the General Chapter which opened on 24 July 1838, Edmund, then aged 76, resigned and was succeeded by Brother Michael Paul Riordan. Three days of heated discussion were devoted to pay-schools, and at the end a somewhat watery compromise was agreed to. It was that because of the financial difficulties facing them, the Brothers of two Dublin schools – at Hanover Street and Mill Street – be allowed 'to receive from the children of easy circumstances such sums as they may feel disposed to give in order to enable the Brothers uphold these establishments'. It was made clear, however, that the principle of the pay-school idea had not been approved by the Chapter, and the new Superior General left no one in any doubt that he was totally opposed to it.

Brother Riordan did nothing to encourage the Hanover Street and Mill Street houses to put the Chapter decision into operation; rather the reverse, but despite his coldness, pay departments came into being in September 1838, with pupils required to pay £1 per quarter. Eighty attended in a room set aside in Hanover Street and forty-three in the monastery parlour in Mill Street, and the development was greeted with particular pleasure by Archbishop Murray. But the issue was by no means settled. Clarification from Rome was necessary and when Brother Riordan belatedly sought the views of the Holy See, he was pointedly biased in his approach. The majority of the Brothers were against pay-schools, he wrote, and he made it clear that he did not support the Chapter's decision. He added that he 'agreed with those Brothers who thought that the measure was an innovation contrary to the letter and spirit of the intention they had when they embraced the Institute'.

Rome's ruling was that the terms of the Papal Brief must be adhered to, especially those relating to gratuitous instruction, and Edmund Rice could have heard of the decision only with feelings approaching dismay. The pay-school proposal had, however, powerful supporters, and Archbishop Murray was one of them. As coadjutor and subsequently successor to Archbishop Troy who died in 1823, he established a very fine reputation as an administrator, a man of action deeply concerned with the welfare of the poor. His influence in Rome was undoubted.

A native of Arklow, Dr Murray was consecrated coadjutor in 1809. The archdiocese was in a very depressed state at the time, with only one hundred or so priests to cater for more than 200,000 Catholics. There was no seminary and education was almost entirely in the hands of Protestants. Roughly fifty Catholic schools catered for 1,300 boys and there were no more than eight free institutions with an aggregate enrolment of fewer than 260. Dr Murray applied himself with tireless zeal to the many problems that existed: he was responsible for the building, at a cost of £80,000, of the Pro-Cathedral which was consecrated in 1825, and when that project was completed, he devoted himself with renewed energy to the provision of educational facilities. The Kildare Place Society, which had been set up in 1811 and quickly became suspect as a proselytising agency, was getting liberal financial assistance from public funds, and in Dr Murray's own parish of St Andrew's, roughly 1,000 of the 3,000 Catholic children of school-going age were attending Protestant schools, while the remainder were getting no education at all. At the time of Dr Murray's death in 1853, Dublin had ninety-seven churches, and approximately two hundred schools were operating in forty-eight parishes.

The contribution by the Christian Brothers to this vastly improved situation was enormous: their first school was opened at Hanover Street in 1812, and others followed in James's Street, Jervis Street, Mill Street and North Richmond Street. Dr Murray had welcomed the Brothers and given them every possible assistance and encouragement; he wanted more and more schools, whether they were free or not, and Edmund Rice's Institute was a powerful instrument in helping him attain his objective. As will be seen, Edmund incurred Dr Murray's displeasure on a matter of principle relating to the National System of Education introduced by the British government, but there were strong mutual bonds of admiration and respect between them, and on the pay-school question, they were in full agreement. 'The rich have high-schools and colleges, and the poor have free schools, but my dear middle-class people, where can they send their children?', Dr Murray wrote.

His question was answered, in part, by the Hanover Street and Mill Street pay departments, but the decision of the Holy See and the intractable opposition of Br Riordan put their future at risk. The Superior of Mill Street, who favoured pay-schools, was replaced in 1840 by one who was opposed, and it became clear that the department would be closed unless something was done. To prevent this, a number of senior Brothers sent a memorial to Rome in which they stated that, of the eighteen houses founded by the Institute, only five had certain funds for their maintenance. Not for the first time, or the last, did the Vatican hear of conflict within the Institute, for the document pointed out that despite a Chapter decision and the approval of Dr Murray, 'Michael Paul Riordan, the person now holding office as Superior General, openly discourages these schools.' The memorial requested a Brief making it lawful to retain the two Dublin pay-schools, and Dr Murray strongly endorsed the appeal in a postscript.

A favourable response eventually arrived from Rome, but it did not end the dissention. At a Chapter held in 1841, the pay-school question was again debated at length, and a subsequent letter informed Dr Murray: 'We conscientiously feel bound not to avail ourselves of the privilege which our Most Holy Father has been pleased to grant (in allowing the two Dublin departments to remain open). We are led to this conclusion, first, because the vast majority of the Brothers have a decided aversion to teach in schools in which payment is received. . . .' Friction was growing, and in an effort to keep the Mill Street pay department open, Brother Francis Ryan went to the extreme of removing the desks to a site in Camden Street. Other Dublin Brothers petitioned the Holy See to be allowed to remove themselves from under the jurisdiction of Br Riordan and place themselves under that of Archbishop Murray.

By that time, Br Riordan had ordered the closure of both pay departments, and when the director of Hanover Street asked for a six-week reprieve because some pupils had paid fees in advance, his request was refused. The Hanover Street establishment was in such difficulties as a result that the community was reduced to living 'on potatoes and buttermilk for breakfast and dinner', and following further representations, the Holy See stepped in once again. Cardinal Franzoni wrote to Br Riordan that 'His Holiness and the Sacred Congregation could not but be greatly surprised that these schools were recently closed against the wishes of the Archbishop of

Dublin. Therefore His Holiness has decided this evil must be remedied without delay. Accordingly he has ordered us to write to you to see to it that the schools in question, which were closed with excessive haste, be re-opened forthwith.' The directive was complied with, but elements of division and ill-feeling inevitably remained.

At this time, Edmund Rice was living in retirement at Mount Sion, and because of his age and the state of his health, he took no active part in the controversy. Had he been Superior General and in good physical condition, there is little doubt that his practical arguments and his powerful influence would have carried a majority of the Brothers in favour of a development which he considered necessary from the early days of his Institute. As it happened, his forward-looking policy was completely vindicated in time: a Brief from the Holy See in 1873 gave a new generation of Brothers the right to establish pay-schools wherever they wished.

11

England and Gibraltar

The first expansion of the Institute outside Ireland was at Preston in 1825, and the first in a large industrial city was at Manchester a year later. Following the setting up of St Mary's school in Lloyd Street there, a night school and a Sunday school for adults were formed and Brother Joseph Murphy reported to Dr T. Kirby, Rector of the Irish College, Rome: 'By sending out the poor boys on Sundays to instruct poor people in the lofts in different directions, we were able to impart instruction to about 2,000 each week. So numerous were the conversions that the priests could not conveniently attend to them all.' An opening in London came in 1826 at Gee Street, Soho, and there was a lapse of ten years before the next English house was established in Sunderland. The building, a large room, was provided by the parish priest, Fr Philip Kearney, a native of Westmeath who had visited Edmund Rice at the Irish Generalate and threatened not to leave the room until promised that two Brothers would be made available.

The Sunderland room was soon crowded to capacity and a great many pupils were non-Catholic. A local paper reported: 'Two Irish Monks have 250 Protestant boys in their school and are converting many of them to the Popish religion.' In reference to this, Brother Stephen Carroll wrote in a memoir: 'I found there were but 73 Catholics and all the others were Protestants or what you may like to call them. They all said the same prayers, all received religious instruction after the same manner and all went to the church on Sundays to receive instruction from the local priest. . . . We told their parents we could not teach the Protestant prayers. "No matter", Protestant parents would say, "teach them what you please; we know you will teach them nothing that is not good".'

The first of a number of schools in Liverpool, with its large Irish population, was in operation by the end of 1837, and the *Catholic History of Liverpool* noted that 'without payment or reward save the voluntary offerings of the parents, these cultivated men did a noble work for the poor children of their own race'. In the same year there was a second opening in London, at Wapping in the East End dock area, and St Patrick's school, Soho, had apparently gained an excellent reputation. Regular features of its annual routine were public examinations of the pupils and a dinner at which donations were accepted for the support of the school. The guests included people like the Duke of Norfolk and the Earls of Surrey, Newbury and Shrewsbury. Shrewsbury was interested in education for the poor and wrote to Edmund Rice asking for the assistance of two Brothers for a school he was in the course of building.

These overseas developments were welcomed by Edmund, who had become somewhat pessimistic about the future of the Institute in Ireland for a number of reasons. Without pay-schools, he felt it would be well-nigh impossible to maintain free schools. Begging was the only alternative and nothing could be said in its favour. As a Carmelite priest, Fr Richard J. Colgan put it with excellent clarity in 1838: 'people were already burdened beyond their means with tithes and taxes and the support of the secular and regular clergy, and when the new Poor Law Bill comes into operation, those who now contribute to your support will every year become less inclined to do so, particularly as the schools under the National Board of Education will in all probability increase in number and utility; will educate the poor gratuitously and consequently supercede the necessity of supporting your establishments'. There were, in fact, 1,106 National Board schools in existence in 1836.

By relying for their continued survival on begging, Fr Colgan added, 'your present system as a religious body contains the seeds of its own dissolution at no far distant period. The fact of your giving a religious education to children may prolong your existence for some time in those places where you are already established, but you will not have courage yourselves, nor will you get encouragement to establish new foundations.' He could also have said that, financial considerations apart, some bishops were reluctant to admit to their dioceses a Congregation of lay-religious independent of episcopal control.

These sombre and eminently commonsense considerations were close to the views held by Edmund for some years, but they were not, surprisingly, persuasive enough to sway those in the Institute who were opposed to pay-schools, irrespective of the effect on the future of the Institute. Expansion outside Ireland was therefore a development which had substantial appeal to the Founder.

Towards the end of 1832 he was invited to a meeting with Archbishop Murray, who had received a letter from a Fr J. McEncroe in New South Wales. 'We want very much five or six competent school-masters; each would get about £50 a year. What a blessing if I could procure two or three of Mr Rice's Brothers. Please speak to him.' Because of a shortage of Brothers, Fr McEncroe's plea could not be granted then, or in the following year, when it was repeated. Brothers eventually went to Australia in 1842, but only after the Holy See had added its weight to the requests.

An application from the American hierarchy for the foundation of a school in Baltimore had to be refused in 1832, as did another from the coadjutor Bishop of Upper Canada, Dr Weld. There was no lack of sympathy from Edmund Rice, for he was eager to see the apostolate of Christian education spread wherever there was a ready harvest, but conditions at home were altogether unfavourable. Yet another plea came early in the 1830s from Dr Michael Anthony Fleming, Irish-born Bishop of St John's, Newfoundland, who asked for four Brothers. Edmund would certainly have been delighted to oblige, if only because of the large numbers, including some of his own relatives, whom he knew had emigrated to Newfoundland, but he made the position clear. In a letter to the Superior of Carrick-on-Suir's foundation, where Dr Fleming was staying, he wrote: 'Tell His Lordship that I should feel much pleasure in having it in my power to render him any service whatever . . . but the state of the Institute is such as not to leave me able to spare him one single subject, not to mention four.'

Here again, Edmund's interest in opening pay-schools had a great deal of relevance, for in addition to the other advantages he could see, pay-schools would almost certainly lead to an increase in vocations to his apostolate and to the priesthood. Had there been sufficient Brothers, he would willingly have complied with the applications from various parts of the world, but as matters stood, his hands were tied. It was only when Rome left him with no alternative that he contrived to spare Brothers for work outside the areas to which he was committed. This happened in the case of Gibraltar.

The Holy See contacted Archbishop Murray in 1835 and told him that Cardinals of the Sacred Congregation had been 'deeply impressed' by the constant requests of the many Irish Catholics who formed part of the Gibraltar garrison, 'and in order that the Catholics and their children may have all the necessary spiritual aid and instruction, the Cardinals have decreed that one or two priests, experienced preachers, be procured from Ireland, and at the same time, one or two Christian Brothers'. After the directive had been brought to Edmund Rice's notice, he selected Brothers Patrick O'Flaherty and Mark Thomas Anthony for the mission, and they departed on 28 October 1835. Dr Murray had supplied them with books and school requisites, and paid all travelling expenses. The Brothers, according to Edmund, 'were to be immediately under the fostering care and protection of the Holy See and the Vicar Apostolic', but they soon discovered that a Committee of Elders considered itself in charge of all financial and school arrangements.

When the school opened in February 1836, the Elders insisted that poor pupils be segregated from the others who would be charged fees – something which was contrary to Institute policy – and lacking on-the-spot advice from his Superior, Brother O'Flaherty unwillingly agreed to a compromise: there would be two schools, with pupils attending one or the other according to amounts voluntarily contributed. It was an unsatisfactory arrangement, but the school was an instant success, at least in terms of the numbers that turned up for instruction.

A report from Gibraltar carried in the *London and Dublin Orthodox Journal* was noticeably gleeful in its tone: 'A Catholic School has been established, the first ever formed since the Rock came into the possession of the English. The school is entrusted to the care of that excellent order of men, the Brothers of the Christian Doctrine. Already upwards of 300 boys have been placed in their charge and did room admit they would soon have over 500. There was a Methodist school which 80 Catholic boys attended, but the appearance of the Christian Brothers has completely upset the swaddling pedagogue and the poor fellow was so enraged at the loss of his scholars that in a fit of frenzy, he determined to make up his loss by crossing the Spanish line where he obtained a room to preach "the true word" to the benighted Spaniards.'

Things were not running smoothly, however. The Brothers quite wrongly followed the Irish school hours of 9 a.m. to 3 p.m., with a half-hour break, whereas the Gibraltar custom was 9 a.m. to midday, with a siesta before resumption at 3 p.m. to 5 p.m. As the Brothers were not sufficiently fluent in Spanish, there was a language barrier, and another cause of contention related to holidays. Brother O'Flaherty wanted his usual summer vacation but the Committee of Elders ruled that as the school had been in existence for only four to five months, the summer holiday should be omitted. Brother O'Flaherty was so annoyed by the interference of the Elders that he threatened that he and his colleague would return to Dublin.

When Edmund Rice was informed of the situation, he ordered the Brothers 'not to abandon their post without directions to do so'. Through his brother, Father John Rice, he complained in very strong terms to the Sacred Congregation about the attitude of both the Elders and the Vicar Apostolic, who apparently had not been very sympathetic to the Brothers, and he intimated that if matters did not improve, the Brothers would be recalled.

The Sacred Congregation was firm in its reaction. It suggested that the grievances of the Brothers were trivial and, evidently briefed by the Vicar Apostolic, Monsignor John B. Zino, listed causes of disagreement: (1) that the Brothers were unwilling to study Spanish 'which is as easy to learn as it is serviceable and indispensable for the progress of the children in the schools', and (2) 'that the Brothers are requiring a greater number of holidays than seems right'. The Sacred Congregation advised Edmund that 'in the heat of argument on these matters it could quite easily happen that something discourteous might be said which a too fervent imagination might regard as a serious insult', and it asked him to exhort the Brothers 'to be docile and respectful to the Vicar established by the Holy See, and to discharge their duties with greater alacrity and zeal, and not slothfully'.

A letter was also sent to Monsignor Zino urging him to work for harmony, but while the passing of the long, hot summer had eased the immediate crisis, nothing had changed fundamentally. Next year the Elders considered a week at Easter and ten days at Christmas would suffice as regards holidays, and they showed no sign of ending their interference in the general running of the school.

Edmund Rice was not one to tolerate outside interference in Institute affairs at home, and he was much less likely to tolerate it from the Elders in Gibraltar. 'You can tell the Elders', he wrote to Brother O'Flaherty, 'that you are to have the usual vacation in some part of July or August, and should they refuse or not be content with this, write to me immediately, and in the meantime, take the vacation yourselves, and do not go to school for them. Whatever answer the Elders give you about the vacation, etc., write to me. However, have courage; the good seed will grow up in the children's hearts later on. . . .' When Brother O'Flaherty told Monsignor Zino the substance of the letter, he was not reassuring and replied that the vacation requested would be most prejudicial to the school.

Meanwhile, Brother Mark Thomas Anthony had become ill, and Brother O'Flaherty closed the school, but promised to re-open it before the end of the normal summer vacation if Brother Anthony's health improved. The Elders reacted decisively: they would not permit any further interference with their school, they said, and they added that they had already taken measures to procure new teachers from

England. In the circumstances, the two Brothers took the first opportunity to leave, and arrived back in Dublin in the middle of August 1837.

The Gibraltar mission had turned out to be a fiasco, and there were faults on all sides. Institute-operated schools were free of outside interference, but the Elders would not accept this. Local customs concerning siestas and vacations had been long established, but the Brothers tended to ignore them. It is clear that the Brothers were not capable of teaching through Spanish, and it may have been true that they showed little inclination to improve their knowledge of the language.

When they arrived home, Edmund Rice left the Brothers in no doubt of his displeasure that they had not made a better effort, but in a letter to Fr Rice and, through him to the Sacred Congregation, he gave them his full support and defended their actions. The Institute had been led to believe that it would be under the protection of the Holy See and its Vicar in Gibraltar, he said, but had been deceived: this was altogether clear from the fact that a body of laymen called Elders took it upon themselves 'to dismiss the Brothers from the schools without even consulting the Holy See or without the consent of the Vicar Apostolic; and this they did because these religious obeyed me, their Superior, in taking a few days' relaxation at a time when even the common feelings of humanity, as well as the common custom of Europe, would demand it from them, and when there could be no evil whatever attending it.'

Archbishop Murray, who originally had acted as intermediary with Edmund, was not pleased with how things had ended and in a letter to Dr Paul Cullen in Rome expressed his annoyance: 'I suppose the Sacred Congregation has been informed that the Elders of Gibraltar have dismissed, most unceremoniously dismissed, the Brothers of the Christian Schools. Religion can have very little chance of thriving in that garrison as long as this faction is allowed to have the management of its religious concerns. It is, I fear, unfortunately true that there is but little piety among the people, and if you except poor Fr Meehan (who had gone from Dublin at the request of the Holy See), little zeal among the clergy.'

Whether or not the experience of the Christian Brothers had anything to do with it, subsequent events in Gibraltar make an interesting footnote. The Vicar Apostolic was replaced and a Dublin Franciscan priest, Fr Henry Hughes, was appointed Bishop. He saw fit to take over the administration of Church funds, and the Elders had him arrested because they considered this a breach of contract. When Daniel O'Connell heard of the arrest, he protested to the British Government, and the Duke of Wellington in his capacity as Prime Minister ordered his immediate release.

The Gibraltar affair was not a propritious start to the Institute's expansion outside Ireland and Britain. It was a failure, but much valuable experience was gained from it. More adequate guarantees of control would be sought in future missions and Institute procedures, enshrining Edmund Rice's vision, would be properly safeguarded. Gibraltar may have exposed a failure to take proper measures to cope with language and climatic problems, but it also showed Edmund's strength of purpose and his loyalty to the Brothers he assigned to undertake a duty which was more difficult than he, or they, imagined.

12

Emancipation and National Education

The capacity to think clearly and to apply a precise, down-to-earth rationale to the attainment of his objectives was one of Edmund Rice's outstanding traits. It undoubtedly helped him achieve the pre-eminent position which was his when he was running a large Waterford business enterprise, and it also was a dominant feature of his role as a religious, a visionary and an educationalist. Pay-schools may not have fitted into a rigid interpretation of Papal Brief terms, but he saw in them material advantages which would in no way compromise the basic purpose of the Institute he founded, or the ideals which inspired those who dedicated their lives to it. The National System of Education was, however, an entirely different matter. It, too, offered material advantages, but it also posed a threat to the religious element which was fundamental to Edmund's approach to how the youth of Ireland should be equipped and moulded.

He wanted to transfer the Generalate of the Institute from Waterford to Dublin for a number of reasons. One was that the Brothers were becoming increasingly active in the capital, and another was that, in dramatic contrast to ordinaries like Dr Walsh and Dr Kelly, he had a sympathetic and supportive friend in Archbishop Murray. 'All the Brothers have been requested to offer prayers to Almighty God, and in a particular manner during the retreat, to procure for us a suitable place for the purpose, so that you will please to join your prayers with the rest until God is pleased to hear us', he wrote in a letter of 1826. It was typical of him to place his trust in Providence. The purpose to which he referred was a proposed foundation in Dublin that would embrace a Generalate, a novitiate and a school.

The prayers were answered, for a vacant lot at North

Richmond Street on the North Circular Road was found two years later. It formed part of the estate of Viscount Mountjoy, Earl of Blessington, which had been leased to a Samuel Scott, and it was acquired on behalf of the Brothers for a term of 980 years at an annual rent of £55 and a sum of £210 for delivery of the deed. The foundation stone was laid by Daniel O'Connell on 9 June 1828 in the presence of a crowd estimated to number 100,000. The Liberator called his old and dear friend, Edmund Rice, 'patriarch of the Monks of the West' in his address, and described the occasion as 'a great day for Ireland'.

Some years later when O'Connell was in prison after impeachment by the British government, he told Brother Austin Dunphy, who visited him: 'I expect much from that school and the teaching of your brotherhood. Never was sound Catholic teaching more needed than at present. The education the government gives is not genuine. It contains a grain of good quality mixed with a bushel that is spurious. Education, to be suited to this country, must be Catholic and Irish in its tone, having as its motto Faith and Fatherland. All engaged in education of the young should remember that "as the twig is bent so the tree inclines".' O'Connell was speaking Edmund Rice's language.

The North Richmond Street complex was another cause of trouble and anxiety to Edmund. Because of a lack of funds, its construction was delayed and work had to be suspended totally in 1829 because no money was available to meet the bills. Fund-raising campaigns in Dublin and England brought some relief, however, and on 23 June 1831, with three senior Brothers and four novices, Edmund moved to North Richmond Street from Hanover Street, which had been a temporary Generalate since March 1828. Next day, Archbishop Murray blessed the buildings, and on 4 July the school opened. The provision of a water supply is typical of one of the niggling problems he faced: the management of the Dublin Water Pipe committee refused to make available a free supply, and when Edmund made an offer to pay, the fee was so exorbitant that it could not be met. Instead, a well had to be sunk on the site and, fortunately, an ample supply was assured. The foundation which would become celebrated as O'Connell School had become a reality.

During the period in question, there were other problems occupying the minds of Edmund Rice and his Brothers and, indeed, that of Daniel O'Connell. The Emancipation movement was gathering such strength that the Duke of Wellington, the English prime minister, and Sir Robert Peel, leader of the House of Commons, were forced to the conclusion that the demand for more rights for Catholics could no longer be postponed. But the draft of a proposed Emancipation bill contained many penal clauses, particularly in relation to religious orders of men, and while some glaring injustices were to be removed, or eased, discriminatory provisions were also included, probably to placate the bigotry of those who opposed giving Catholics the rights to which they were entitled.

An assembly of Brothers held its first session the day the Act of Emancipation received the grudging assent of King George IV, and much time was devoted to considering the implications of the legislation. One of the provisions decreed banishment for life in respect of 'any person admitted to a religious order', for instance. In the House of Commons, the Duke of Wellington had made his intolerant position clear when he said: 'There is no man more convinced than I am of the absolute necessity of carrying into execution that part of the present measure which has for its object the extinction of monastic orders in the country.' The situation as far as the Brothers were concerned was not favourable.

Before the Brothers gathered for the assembly, Edmund Rice had exhorted them: 'Be intent on prayer, and whatever may happen will turn to our good. Cast all your cares into the arms of divine Providence, and in union with your thousands of pupils, join in fervent prayer and supplication to our divine Lord and to Mary, Help of Christians, to save our Congregation from this impending calamity.' Prayer was, to Edmund Rice, the most powerful of all weapons in times of crisis, but in this instance, there was strong support, even from Protestants, for the Institute. A petition to Parliament that the Christian Brothers should be exempt from penal clauses was presented by 'The Protestant Gentry and Inhabitants of the City of Waterford'. It stated that if the Congregation was suppressed 'it would deprive thousands of poor, destitute children of education and clothing, blessings so much wanted in this country'.

In a similar vein, a memorial was forwarded by the Marquis of Lansdowne on behalf of 'The Protestant Gentry and Inhabitants of Carrick-on-Suir and Vicinity in the County of Tipperary'. Signed by the Rev. Stanish Grady, vicar of Carrick, it paid tribute to the work done by the Brothers and the beneficial results evident among poor children. The Marquis of Lansdowne wrote to Edmund Rice that the Lord Chancellor was of the opinion that the Brothers would not come under the penal clauses because they were not subject to a foreign superior, but the greatest morale-booster came from the formidable Daniel O'Connell. As acting counsel for the Franciscans, he wrote that 'though the law is insolent enough in its pretensions, it will be, and must be, totally inefficient in practice: it is almost impossible that any prosecutions should be instituted at all, and it is quite impossible that any prosecution should be successful.'

Whatever fears the Brothers may have had were surely allayed when Edmund Rice read O'Connell's opinion to the assembly. It was prudently decided, however, that in accordance to one of the legislative clauses, the Brothers would register as required with a Clerk of Peace, but under protest. The returns, published by order of the House of Commons in 1830, showed that there were fifty-five Brothers in fourteen houses.

With the worries of the North Richmond Street foundation and the Emancipation Act out of the way, Edmund Rice became involved in yet another troublesome and controversial matter. In this, and not for the first time, he showed an immense strength of character and an uncompromising commitment to spirituality as a vital requisite in a fully-rounded education. A Royal Commission was established in 1824 to investigate the state of education in Ireland, the population of which was then roughly 7,000,000. A system which had been promoted so that 'children of Popish natives may become Protestant and English' – as the Charity School Society had declared its objective – had failed dismally, and something new was called for. The Commission showed a marked bias in its composition for, in an overwhelmingly Catholic country, it was made up of four Protestants and one Catholic. Not surprisingly, it did not look with any great favour on Catholic education.

As a result of its recommendations, the Chief Secretary for Ireland, E. G. Stanley, laid a plan for a 'System of National Education' before the House of Commons in 1831, and in October of the same year, the Duke of Leinster was invited to head a Board which would supervise its operation. The Board members appointed a couple of months later were Archbishop Murray, Dr Richard Whately, Protestant Archbishop of Dublin, the Rev. Dr Sadlier, Provost of Trinity College, Robert Holmes, a Protestant government official, the Rev. Mr Carlisle, a Scottish Presbyterian, and Anthony Richard Blake, a Catholic. The Board, like the Commission, showed a notable imbalance in its composition.

The new system proposed interdenominational education, offering combined literary but separate religious instruction. The plan was opposed by numbers of Anglicans and Presbyterians who were against Catholics being given any share at all of available funds and, on the Catholic side, there were mixed views. Dr Murray was in favour, and so were other prominent personalities like Dr Crolly, Catholic Archbishop of Armagh, Daniel O'Connell and Dr Doyle (JKL), Bishop of Kildare and Leighlin. Dr John McHale, Archbishop of Tuam, and the first Irish bishop who had not gone abroad to be educated since the Reformation, emerged as a redoubtable opponent.

Because there were restrictions on religious instruction, Edmund Rice distrusted the proposals from the beginning, but he exercised his usual prudence and caution before coming to a decision. The system would bring material benefits, such as grants-in-aid for the erection and furnishing of schools, and there would also be a capitation grant – a very modest one of £10 per annum for every 100 pupils on the rolls, or 2/– per pupil per year. But meagre as the benefits were, they would be a considerable help to those schools which depended on house-to-house begging, or the occasional charity sermon, for their continued existence.

Edmund had a number of discussions with Archbishop Murray, who advised him to bring the Institute's schools into the system, and after consultations with the Brothers, he decided to apply for admission of six schools on an experimental basis – North Richmond Street and Mill Street in Dublin, Mount Sion and St Patrick's in Waterford, and establishments in Dungarvan and Ennistymon. According to the terms of the system, the schools would be open to visits by inspectors who would examine the pupils and report on their progress.

That was fair enough, but other conditions placed severe restrictions on the saying of prayers and the display of religious objects, both of which were matters dear to Edmund Rice's heart. In addition, involvement in the system entailed the use of text-books prescribed by the National Education Board.

A sample from one of these is extremely interesting insofar as it reveals the mentality of the system's administrators and their quite cavalier contempt for Irish ethnic sentiments. In the *Third Book of Lessons* compiled by Mr Carlisle, the Scottish Presbyterian clergyman who was a member of the Board, and issued in 1835, there was a hymn which pupils were expected to learn and sing. One verse went:

> I thank the goodness and the grace
> That on my birth have smiled,
> And made me in these Christian days
> A happy English child.

In 1838, Archbishop Whately revised this text-book, but while the second edition omitted several pieces of prose and poems which had a native flavour, such as references to the harp and harpers, the 'happy English child' hymn was retained.

There were some aspects of participation which must have caused Edmund and the Brothers in general a deal of satisfaction. One inspector, John F. Murray, reported after a visit to North Richmond Street that 'it is quite enough for an inspector to say that he observes in this excellent institution everything to admire and nothing to condemn. . . . The inspector abstains from giving any suggestions as he cannot see how the present excellent management could be improved.'

The Rev. George Dwyer, a Protestant rector, was equally laudatory. Having been to fifty schools on inspection, he wrote: 'I would say the most perfect schools I have ever been in in my life were the schools in Mill Street in Dublin and the (Brothers') schools in Cork; the most extraordinary progress I ever saw made by children, the most admirable adaptation of the information to be communicated to the peculiar bent and genius and disposition of the child, a sifting and a searching of what the future destination of the child was, and an application of instruction to that destination – a most curious eliciting and drawing forth and development of the powers of the children.' The Rev. Dwyer was amazed at the numbers of pupils in Waterford and Dungarvan schools and added: 'the peculiar reputation and sanctity of the schools attracted (the children) from ten and fifteen miles distant.'

The Rev. Mr Dwyer's reactions are of much interest. They show that in the Schools he listed there was clearly a substantial amount of attention paid to elements of education which became an integral part of enlightened schooling more than a century later – aptitude testing and career guidance. It is not generally recognised that in concerning themselves with such matters, the Christian Brothers showed a strikingly intelligent, imaginative and down-to-earth approach which was many years before its time. In doing so, they upheld to the full the spiritual quality so vital to Edmund Rice's vision, as is seen in the Rev. Dwyer's reference to the schools' 'peculiar reputation and sanctity'.

But Edmund's misgivings about the system were to prove well-founded. The text-books at first prescribed, while a special series was being prepared, were those of the Kildare Place Society, and when the new books became available – thirteen in all – not one was compiled either by a Catholic or by an Irish person. Irish history and literature were ignored, and some of the works included essays on religious subjects by Archbishop Whately and other prominent Protestant divines. The books brought out by the Christian Brothers were, according to an inspector, 'not such as they can sanction in a national school for general instruction'.

Some of the Board's officials were determined to apply with complete rigour the rules relating to religious practices, and those who visited schools were questioned as to whether the pupils had been found saying the Ave Maria or making the

Sign of the Cross. While the display of religious pictures or statues was considered a breach of the rules, the Board did not insist on their removal 'provided the images and pictures are completely screened during the hours of general education'. A Captain William Wellesley reported that in a school run by the Christian Brothers in Dublin, he saw 'a very objectionable prayer-card' hanging over the chimney-piece. 'There was some device upon the top of the card', he noted, 'and the Virgin's name was mentioned towards the end of it, and as I know that the Roman Catholics used the Virgin in their prayers, I thought it was very objectionable. I mentioned it to the Superior of Schools, who appeared very sorry and surprised to hear of its being there, and assured me that it would be taken away.'

In the Dungarvan Christian Brothers' school an inspector took a catechism which he found in a desk and threw it on the floor saying 'That has no right to be here', while at Mount Sion, an official who insisted on speaking to a class against the Immaculate Conception had to be forcibly removed. As instances of this nature grew in number, the Brothers and Catholic teachers in general used subterfuge: prayers were recited when it was safe to do so, and religious objects were removed only when news of an inspector's approach became known.

The situation became increasingly intolerable in the case of the Brothers' schools, where a crucifix and an image of Our Lady were traditionally displayed, and where the custom of saying a short prayer whenever the clock struck the hour was entrenched. Edmund Rice was kept informed of what was happening and did not like what he heard. He decided to call an extraordinary General Chapter to discuss the position, and it met for its first session on 27 December 1836. It quickly became obvious that there was a serious gulf between the ideals of the Institute and the purpose of the system. On the one hand, a rule of the Institute stated that 'the Brothers are to recollect that the instruction of children in piety and religion is the great and main end of their Institute. That is to be their first and principal care in regard to their pupils.' On the other hand, the system gave secular education the first and chief place, prohibited the display of religious emblems and the incidental teaching of Catholic doctrine and, in leaving religious instruction a matter of choice to managers, suggested to children 'that religion is a matter of secondary importance and may even be laid aside altogether at discretion'.

Recommendations to the Board for changes favourable to Catholic schools were rejected and Archbishop Whately stated the reason with great frankness when he wrote: 'The schools in Roman Catholic districts will be so many Maynooths, so many hot-beds of bigotry and religious animosity. . . . I believe that mixed (undenominational) education is gradually enlightening the mass of the people, and if we give it up, we give up the only hope of weaning the Irish from the abuses of popery.' He added, rather more hopefully than factually, that the 'education supplied by the National Board is gradually undermining the vast fabric of the Irish Roman Catholic church'.

The dilemma facing Edmund Rice was a very real one. There were the monetary advantages offered by the national system and there was acceptance of it by distinguished Catholic prelates, including his friend, Archbishop Murray. But there was the undeniable conflict of interest between the Board and the Institute. The extraordinary General Chapter decided that a continued connection with the National Board 'would ultimately prove fatal to the religious as well as to the professed object of the Institute', and appointed a five-member committee to investigate the resources of the schools involved, with a direction that, where independent survival was possible, the links should be severed. After the committee had carried out its work, it recommended that Mount Sion, North Richmond Street and Mill Street should be withdrawn, but it was felt that Dungarvan, St Patrick's and Ennistymon could not remain in existence without aid. They were, however, exhorted to do everything possible, as quickly as possible, to bring about a situation in which the inhibiting influences of the system would play no part.

The decision to remove Mount Sion, Mill Street and North Richmond Street was courageous in view of the extreme poverty of the Institute as a whole and, indeed, in view of the pro-system attitudes of powerful Catholic figures, cleric and lay, but it was in keeping with the manner in which – imbued with Edmund Rice's vision – the Brothers adhered to ideals and principals. It was Edmund's function to report the development to Dr Murray. In doing so he was brief and to the point. Having communicated the decision he added: 'If this step should be disagreeable to Your Grace, I shall be very sorry for it.' Dr Murray showed that the step was certainly disagreeable: despite years of friendship with, and support for, Edmund Rice, he uncharacteristically withdrew his annual donation of £40 to the Hanover Street school, but it was a temporary exercise of his displeasure and he may have been motivated by chagrin that he was not informed in advance of the action the Brothers took.

The system of national education became an issue of public controversy between Dr Murray and Archbishop McHale, and it was discussed at length by the Sacred Congregation of Propaganda which, having first denounced it, later adopted a neutral stance by leaving participation 'to the prudent discretion of each bishop'. Eventually the Board moved away from its original rigidity concerning religious instruction and the hopes of Archbishop Whately were not realised.

The withdrawal of the Christian Brothers – all their schools were taken out in later years – was a major factor in the evolution of a new approach, and when referring to altered circumstances in 1900, Archbishop William Walsh of Dublin was mindful of the example given by Edmund Rice and his colleagues. 'I am convinced' he said, 'that no one who gives thought to it can fail to recognise that at least one important factor in the working-out of that far-reaching change has been the unflinching determination of our Catholic people to stand by the Christian Brothers with the same steadfastness with which the Christian Brothers stand by the great fundamental principle of their Institute.'

13

Internal Divisions

From the time Edmund Rice initiated his apostolate, there was scarcely a month in which he did not have to face external obstacles and difficulties. They ranged from financial problems and cholera epidemics to the hostile workings of the political system and the occasional opposition of bishops and priests. Through his astuteness, practicality and tact, and through his simple and profound belief in the efficacy of prayer, he contrived to keep the Institute afloat. More than that, he consolidated the foundations so that future expansion would be possible, no matter how formidable the odds. But there were other difficulties and they were potentially more damaging, and certainly more painful, because they were internal. It was not all plain sailing and harmony within the growing Congregation. Individuality and a tendency to rebel against authority – peculiar Irish characteristics perhaps – asserted themselves, and the control exercised by the Founder came under question and attack, so much so that the continued survival of the Institute was sometimes in doubt.

Up to the receipt of the Papal Brief, the Brothers followed the rule adopted by the Presentation nuns, with some modifications, but after the Brief had been accepted at the 1822 Chapter, a special commission was set up to draft a new code of regulations which would be ready for the General Chapter, due ten years later. Meanwhile, a temporary set of rules based on those of the De La Salle Congregation in France, were observed. The De La Salle Order had been in existence for more than a century. Founded by St John Baptist De La Salle, it had been given a Papal Brief by Pope Benedict XIII in 1724, and the Institute had much to learn from its lengthy experience. Both Congregations were alike in that they were

composed of male religious dedicated to the Christian education of the poor, and while the Briefs issued to both were
largely similar, they were not identical.

A small minority of Institute members chose not to accept
the Brief in 1822 because they felt, conscientiously no doubt,
that they should remain under the jurisdiction of the local
ordinary. The great majority, however, chose to place
themselves under the protection of the Holy See and under the
authority of a Superior General, the post to which Edmund
was elected by the Directors of the Foundations then in existence. In the years that followed, however, it became apparent that there was some dissatisfaction with the manner in
which the Institute was being run: Edmund's generalship was
criticised for being too autocratic and there were demands for
a greater degree of democracy. There were calls for the right
to vote to be extended to include other than Superiors and for
four Assistants to be appointed instead of two as the terms of
the Brief stipulated. Agitation for the holding of a second
Chapter at which these changes could be made increased.

Edmund Rice was opposed to holding a Chapter and his
opposition only added to the resentment which the exercise of
his authority had already generated. The resentment was not
widespread. Instead it was concentrated in one particular
house, the North Monastery, Cork, and articulated by one
person there, Brother Joseph Leonard. In letters to the
Superior General of the De La Salles and to priest friends, he
made his feelings known, and there can be no doubt that on
the home front he sought to influence as many Brothers as
possible towards accepting his opinions. He was not averse to
misstatement or exaggeration in promoting support for his
opinions as when in December 1828 he wrote in a letter to
Paris that Edmund 'is in a very pitiable condition. His mind is
so disordered that he is completely incapable of applying
himself to the business of the Institute.'

He went on to say that Edmund 'was inclined to set himself
against the view of the two Assistants in all matters concerning the welfare of the Institute. He even said to them very
often that he would not listen to any remonstrance of theirs
and that he was not obliged to follow their advice unless it
agreed with his own opinions. His mind has been thus

deranged for a long time. . . . It seems to me that his illness will be of very long duration.' In another letter he wrote that 'the Brothers want so much to settle several matters regarding the nature and stability of the Institute that they are determined to assemble.'

Brother Leonard's reference to an alleged mental breakdown suffered by Edmund Rice was obviously based on a rumour which had no substance in fact, but which nevertheless spread and would continue to arise in succeeding years. One of Edmund's Assistants, Brother Austin Dunphy, described it as a 'false and very mischievous story', but the most concrete refutation came from Edmund's own performance during the period in question. He had been physically ill in the latter part of 1828 – he was then aged 66 – but he was sufficiently alert mentally to insist that a General Chapter was not necessary because one was due according to rule, in 1831–2, and an ordinary assembly of Brothers would suffice to transact whatever business was necessary without, as he put it, 'going to the expense and inconvenience' involved in summoning a full General Chapter. He also consulted Father Peter Kenney, Superior of the Jesuits, on the matter, and his opinion was that a Chapter should not be held until it was legally due.

Yet the pressure to call a Chapter grew and Edmund reluctantly yielded to it. 'My consent was rather extorted from me', he explained, for notwithstanding his own attitude and the opinion of Father Kenney, 'through the workings of a few individuals, the rest of the professed Brothers got rather clamorous so that I was obliged to submit'. This approach shows little sign of mental instability, but it would have been better had he stuck to his guns, for the Chapter which took place in 1829 achieved nothing to the benefit of the Institute. On the contrary, it created acrimony and, as was later established, it was uncanonical in its constitution and invalid in its decisions.

It was an occasion of dissention, squabbling and internal politics, and it was a very distressing event for Edmund. The Chapter was composed of thirty in all between directors of schools and professed Brothers. Its make-up was not in conformity with the Brief, and dissatisfaction with the Superior

The Edmund Rice icon by Raymond Kyne

Statue of Edmund Rice by Peter Grant at Callan

General's authority quickly became evident when a proposal was made that he should not be permitted to make propositions or recommend amendments on the ground that he would exercise too great an influence. He would be reduced to a mere figurehead, a status he very properly refused to accept. The meeting went on to elect two extra Assistants who would not reside in the Generalate and this was clearly a ploy to dilute centralised authority. It was also a violation of the Brief, and considerable deviousness was employed to accomplish it, because crucial information supplied by the De La Salle Superior General was withheld from the assembly.

In this matter, Edmund Rice allowed himself to be led astray somewhat too easily. The Brief was quite explicit in its regulations regarding those entitled to vote and the number of Assistants permitted, but perhaps spurious guidelines allegedly coming from the De La Salles, and communicated through Brother Joseph Leonard, overcame the doubts he certainly entertained. He was not aware at the time that vital information supplied was not made public.

He was, however, shrewd enough to realise what was afoot, and the situation caused him acute anxiety. In the circumstances, he decided to submit his resignation as Superior General. Kneeling before the Brothers, he read a short statement which he had prepared and withdrew from the room. It was an unexpected and dramatic turn of events, and it caused a great deal of concern both to his critics and supporters. In his absence, the Brothers promptly and unanimously agreed not to accept the resignation, and Edmund was recalled to preside over the remainder of the illegal and regrettable Chapter. It was an intensely unhappy time for him, as he later made clear to the De La Salle Superior General.

'The Chapter produced no good but, on the contrary, for the seeds of independence with the principles subversive of religious discipline as well as the old and good order were sown in it', he wrote. 'Young Brothers were encouraged to come forward to make complaints of their Directors by which their authority and that of those who may succeed them was much lessened.' He asked for guidance concerning his own authority and the appointment of additional Assistants who would be non-residential, and he proceeded to show his displeasure at some of the recommendations made by the Chapter: 'Hitherto the quantity and quality of our food and beverage were both wholesome and sufficient', he explained, 'but in this Chapter a rule was made to increase the quantity by the addition of a supper, not taken before, as our dinner hour is about half past three in the evening; and to alter the quality by the adoption of tea as a general beverage for breakfast; also a certain description of cotton cloth which was in general use for about 25 years amongst us was prohibited as being too common and a more genteel and expensive sort of woollen cloth was introduced in its stead.'

Doubtless bearing in mind that tea was very expensive – it was selling at from 6/– to 10/– a lb. – and that the woollen material would mean the expenditure of more money, he wrote that these changes were brought in 'at a time when for want of means of support, we could not take a postulant into the novitiate, and that we were obliged to suspend the work on our building (North Richmond Street), now half-finished, and for want of which four Brothers are obliged to sleep in one chamber detached from the house, exposed to the suffocating heat of summer and the pinching cold of winter. With regard to the two additional Assistants who were evidently brought in for the purpose of checking the authority of the Superior, they have already caused both trouble and inconvenience, but this may have happened for want of knowing the nature of their functions'.

The De La Salle Superior General fully supported Edmund's stand in his reply. All De La Salle Assistants were obliged to live in the Generalate, he stated, and regarding the authority of the Superior General, he went on: 'He should listen to the opinions of his Assistants, and then adopt whatever course seemed best to him, even when such a course has the least support. In cases of very great importance, he ought to reflect seriously for fear of taking a wrong course.' This justified the line Edmund had taken all along, not least during the period of his alleged insanity, but it did not mollify his opponents. If anything, they became more implacable in their opposition and more hardened in what seemed to be personal enmity, especially three from the North Monastery – Brother Joseph Leonard, his brother, John Baptist, and Brother Michael Paul Riordan.

Brother Joseph Leonard was an untiring letter-writer, and towards the end of 1829 he was complaining to the De La Salles that Edmund Rice 'had resolved to pay no attention to the decrees of the Chapter, which was a source of discontent among the brethren'. The De La Salle Superior warned Edmund of the consequences of such action: 'Once a matter has been decided, it should be strictly adhered to and the Superior should be the first to give the example of submission even though he did not approve of the matter decided. His vow of obedience obliges him to do so. If the Superior himself was to infringe the decisions of the Chapter, he would give a bad example which, before long, the Brothers would imitate and soon the observance of the rule and order of the Superior would be no more respected than the decisions of the Chapter. You understand the results of this conduct.'

Edmund understood and wrote to those houses which had received permission to ignore Chapter decisions directing them to observe the decrees forthwith. He also set about ensuring that the Chapter due in 1831–2 would be properly constituted and with this in mind sent a copy of the Papal Brief and the decrees of the 1829 Chapter to three eminent Dublin canonists for their opinions. The replies were unanimous: only the Directors of houses could vote in electing the Superior General and his Assistants, or be admitted to the proceedings. It emerged from this that the 1829 Chapter was uncanonical and, as a consequence, all of its decrees were invalid.

In legal terms the Chapter was proved to have been something in the nature of an unnecessary fiasco. To explain the agitation that led to its reluctant calling, and to understand areas of conflict that developed in ensuing years, it is necessary to revert to earlier years of the Institute's history, even at the risk of repetition. At this point it is, indeed, essential to postulate reasons why some admirable men, especially those of the North Monastery, came to be intransigently at odds with the policy of the one who initiated an apostolate to which they had dedicated themselves with remarkable success.

When he sold all he had and devoted both the proceeds and himself to the education of the illiterate poor, Edmund Rice was not indulging in a mere exercise of philanthropy. He had

in mind, whether he knew it or not, a concept which was completely revolutionary in the Church – a Congregation founded
by a layman. With his few followers, he took temporary, and a
year later, permanent vows, and from the beginning he
showed a determination to get Papal approval for his plans.
While he and his early disciples awaited that approval, they
used amended Presentation Order rules as a disciplinary
guideline for their spiritual regimen. The first Brothers took
their temporary vows in 1808, but it was not until 1816 that
Archbishop Troy secured for Edmund a copy of the Brief
which had been granted to the De La Salles. There is no
evidence that when Edmund embarked on his unheard-of
course he was aware of the existence of the De La Salles, who
at the time when Edmund Rice began his work were fragmen-
tised and almost annihilated by the impact of the French
Revolution.

When Edmund received the De La Salle Brief, he circulated
copies of its articles to every house of his Institute so that
Superiors would have concrete material on which to base
draft proposals for their own Brief. A number of meetings
were held and a proposed constitution was submitted to
Rome. When the Brief was eventually granted, a meeting of
perpetually-professed Brothers was held in Thurles in August
1821 to discuss its terms. Significantly, no one from the North
Monastery attended and this was undoubtedly due to the
hard-line diocesan attitude of the Bishop of Cork. Neither was
there any representative from Cork when the first General
Chapter took place at Mount Sion in January 1822.

The Cork house had been set up in 1811, but its establishment did not take place as a result of Brothers being sent there
by Edmund Rice. Two men had been sent from Cork for
training and spiritual formulation at Mount Sion, and they
were unlikely to share the same deep feeling towards Edmund
as Brothers in other houses which had sprung directly from
Mount Sion. This may have had a substantial bearing on the
fact that opposition to Edmund was largely engineered in,
and orchestrated from, the North Monastery. By the time the
North Monastery came into the mainstream of Institute activity, it is not unreasonable to assume that some of its
members wrongly looked on their Congregation as an offshoot

of the De La Salles, rather than as a uniquely innovative Irish congregation.

In an 1827 letter to the De La Salle Superior General, Brother Joseph Leonard referred to the French Congregation as 'the parent Institute upon which ours is grafted', which suggests that he was only vaguely aware, if at all, of the real origins of Edmund Rice's apostolate, and Brother Michael Paul Riordan subsequently translated a life of Father John Baptist De La Salle adding a chapter devoted to 'the rise of the Institute in Ireland'. This view may have been sincerely and honestly held; it may also cast some light on the painful divergence of attitudes which emerged between Edmund and those who adhered to his spiritually-based but sometimes pragmatic ideas on the one hand, and those who opposed them on the other.

In the matter of pay-schools, for instance, opposition is perfectly understandable in Brothers who chose to look upon their Institute merely as an offshoot of the De La Salle Congregation, which was exclusively committed to gratuitous education. Edmund Rice's visionary concept was, however, less restricted, more embracing and, in the peculiar circumstances of the Ireland of his time, more realistic. It was also more necessary.

At the Thurles meeting of Brothers in 1821 some alterations in the terms of the Brief were suggested. It was proposed that, to provide for a more democratic involvement in the formation of the Institute's government, the right to vote for the Superior General and his Assistants should be extended to all professed Brothers, but when a request was made to Rome, it was not granted. This was not Edmund's fault, and there was nothing he could do about it, facts which do not seem to have been fully recognised or accepted.

The North Monastery chose to come under the Brief in 1826, and it was a courageous decision taken against the strongly-expressed wishes of the Bishop. Had the Cork house been more closely involved in earlier meetings and discussions, subsequent points of conflict might not have arisen, but as it was in the latter part of the 1820s, the relative newcomers from the North Monastery generated the most criticism and dissension.

Brother Joseph Leonard did, however, have an occasional valid point, as when he sought to justify the changes relating to the quality and quantity of food. 'At 8 o'clock we breakfast on bread and tea or coffee', he wrote. 'At 9 o'clock the schools open and in several towns they are about a mile from the house. We stay there without a break until 3 o'clock. At 3:30 we dine on boiled meat (very rarely roast) and vegetables – no bread except on fast days. Now, the only additions we made with regard to food were to allow Brothers 4 oz. of bread and a little milk at 8 o'clock in the evening for supper and to keep for breakfast tea or coffee instead of the porridge which the Superior ordered for the Brothers.'

He claimed, with some justice, that the introduction of supper and the provision of tea at breakfast were reasonable measures for Brothers who had, in many cases, more than 150 pupils in their charge and who were physically exhausted after a day of teaching. Edmund, however, was content to leave the existing austere dietary programme as it was, and in this he was adhering to his personal spirit of asceticism, an element which was, to him, spiritually enriching.

Because of the unhappy experiences of the 1829 Chapter, he was determined that the one due within a couple of years would be both lawful and productive. It opened on 27 December 1831 and, as required, he tendered his resignation as Superior General. In the election that followed, he received eleven of the fourteen eligible votes and two Assistants, rather than four, were chosen. Several important decisions were made in relation to the training of novices, the establishment of a fund for the support of superannuated Brothers and the like. It was agreed to send delegates to study aspects of the De La Salle operation, particularly in regard to novices; there was unanimous support for a proposal to petition Rome for changes in terms of the Brief which would allow a wider participation in Chapters and permit the Superior General to hold office for life, instead of ten years. In heartening contrast to the 1829 assembly, Edmund was pleased with what had been done. Much of the confusion which had arisen was dispelled and the Institute had been placed on a sound constitutional footing.

There was one decision, though, which caused the Founder displeasure. It was that he should sit for his portrait, and this was distasteful to someone who had always shunned the limelight and who, by nature and temperament, was of a very retiring disposition. 'His profound humility was most striking', a colleague, Brother Myles Kelly recorded, 'and this was manifest in his reluctance through life to have his likeness taken.' While he showed his aversion to having his portrait painted, he had to submit in obedience to the Chapter ruling, and it is regrettable that the result was not a success. For whatever reason, the finished work was inferior: it was said to have lacked expression and where it is, or whether it is extant at all, is not known.

The Holy See approved in time of the Chapter petitions, and two Brothers spent three months with the De La Salles in France. Edmund showed his appreciation of the hospitality extended to them. 'Our prayers and the prayers of the brethren shall be offered for your welfare and for the welfare of your Society', he wrote to the Superior General and, as a concrete token of his gratitude, he forwarded a curious present – two cases of razors and twelve pen-knives! Doubtless he had a sympathetic contact in a hardware shop.

Back from France, the Brothers reported that they had seen much to edify them, but they pointed out that differences in race, customs and environment were so great that few of the De La Salle regulations and practices could be introduced with advantage into the Institute novitiate in Ireland. The same, indeed, applied in general terms, and it was readily accepted that the distinctive spirit of the Irish Congregation inculcated by its Founder could only be reflected by distinctive methods of procedure.

The outspoken critic, Brother Joseph Leonard, died before the 1831–32 Chapter took place. He had been in wretched health ('I am in the hands of the doctor – spitting blood every morning – I am to have leeches applied to my chest this evening.'), and suffered bouts of severe depression ('It sometimes occurs to me in my solitude that when a man is not only useless but becomes a burden to society, it should be deemed an act of heroic virtue that he commit suicide.'). His physical condition was probably a major factor in his antipathy towards Edmund who, on at least two occasions, sent him on a holiday to France for the good of his health.

From his letters, Brother Joseph emerged as a sad, discontented and rather pathetic person, but his death did not mean the end of resentment and opposition to Edmund in the North Monastery. Brother John Baptist Leonard and Brother Michael Paul Riordan remained hostile, and the hostility manifested itself in ways that were sometimes remarkably petty in succeeding years. Edmund was at one stage denied a bed in a Dublin house and rumours about his mental incapacity were resurrected. Aspersions were cast on his probity and sense of obedience, and he found little rest or tranquility in his declining years.

He accepted such things without rancour or recrimination. He had enshrined his attitude in a rule which he had exhorted Brothers to take very much to heart: 'For as worldly people love and seek with great diligence honour, fame and high reputation, so they who are spiritual and who seriously follow Christ love and ardently desire the things opposite to them; insomuch that, could it be done without sin, they would willingly suffer contumely, false testimony and injuries and desire to be esteemed as fools (giving no occasion thereto) in order to resemble Jesus Christ, who has given the example, and who is the way, the truth and the life that leads to glory.' That was his philosophy in a nutshell, and he followed it with a quiet and unshakeable doggedness.

14

Legal Irritations

One of the charges often made against Edmund Rice in Ireland and in letters to Rome was that he was frequently embroiled in litigation. The accusations were true: to his considerable irritation and inconvenience, he was an unwilling party to many troublesome and annoying cases, but in every instance, his involvement had one purpose – to protect the interests of others, particularly the poor, the orphaned and the destitute elderly. The pattern started when he was a businessman in Waterford. Because of his reputation for honesty, acumen and integrity, he was made the executor of wills and the trustee of charitable bequests. These roles were thrust upon him. He had quite enough to do without the endless work and worry which such honorary duties imposed on him with increasing regularity.

One early suit, for example, related to a bequest of 1791 which allocated a large sum of money to the poor of Thurles. Edmund was later asked to administer it by the Archbishop of Cashel, and matters were only finalised in 1823 when the two leading Irish barristers, Daniel O'Connell and Lalor Shiel, brought a successful action in the Chancery Court, London. In 1828 a Carrick-on-Suir priest bequeathed £1,000 to the local Brothers' school, but the will was contested and a settlement was not reached until 1856 when Edmund was long dead and when, inevitably, most of the estate had been used up in lawyers' fees. In this instance, as in others, difficulties were created because the bequest was given to a Catholic charity and, therefore, subject to penal clauses still in force.

One such clause was invoked against the will of Mary Power of Waterford, who died in 1804 and left several thousand pounds for the building and maintenance 'of an asylum

for twelve poor ladies'. Bishop John Power was the chief executor, and a nephew of the deceased woman contested the
will. The case came before the Court of Rolls in 1815, with
John Philpot Curran presiding, and his judgment was as important as his summing-up comments were interesting: 'It is
said that this will has been obtained by fraud practised by
"one John Power"', Curran said. 'I see no semblance of fact
to sustain such a charge. Who does this "one John Power a
Popish priest" turn out to be? I found he is a Catholic
clergyman, a doctor of divinity and the Titular Bishop of the
diocese of Waterford. And yet I am now pressed to believe
that this gentleman has obtained the will by fraud. Every fact
now appearing repels the charge; I cannot but say that the
personal character of the person accused repels it still more
strongly. But I am called to interfere, it being a foolish bequest to superstitions, and those Popish ones. I have looked
into those bequests, and I find the object of them is to provide
shelter and comfortable support for poor, helpless females,
and clothes and food and instruction for poor, orphaned
children. Would to God I could see more frequent instances of
such bequests. But these uses are condemned as being not
only superstitious, but Popish ones.'

Curran, a Protestant and father of Sarah Curran, Robert
Emmet's celebrated sweetheart, left no one in doubt as to his
attitude and, indeed, his anger. 'I am aware that this objection means somewhat more than directly meets the ear, if it
means anything', he went on. 'The object of these bequests, it
seems, are Catholics or, as they have been called, Papists, and
the insinuation clearly is that the religion of the objects of this
woman's bounty calls upon me to exercise some peculiar
rigour of interference to abridge or defeat her intention. I
think, therefore, the motion ought to be refused, and I think
myself bound to mark still more strikingly my sense of its
impropriety by refusing it with full costs.'

Following this judgment, it was decreed that all the be-
quests in Mary Power's will should be vested in the Commis-
sioners of Charitable Donations and Bequests, a body of fifty
Protestants which included prelates of the Established
Church, judges and the Provost of Trinity College. Bishop
Power was nominated to act as sole executor, but scarcely had

the arrangements been finalised when he died. Edmund Rice was then appointed administrator by the Attorney General: he could, of course, have demurred, but in exercising his sense of responsibility, he took upon himself a task which caused unbelievable trouble.

The Commissioners were bureaucratic and inefficient; they were also anti-Catholic and, as a result unco-operative. The money involved, £6,400, was invested in a government stock against Edmund's wishes and advice, because the return on it was miserly. It was the function of the official receiver, a Mr Mostyn, to collect the dividends and forward them to the Commissioners' secretary, a Mr Causland. He would then transfer the money to Edmund for distribution, and the method of transfer gives an indication of the amount of unnecessary work created by an astonishingly inept procedure.

Mr Causland cut the banknotes in half and despatched one set of half-notes which Edmund distributed. Having obtained signed receipts and returned them to Dublin, Mr Causland had to forward the second set of half-notes which had to be matched and distributed.

Not satisfied with operating this ludicrous arrangement, Mr Causland later imposed a levy of $2\frac{1}{2}$ per cent on the interest from the investment, but he did not know the calibre of the man he was dealing with. Edmund appealed to the Attorney General, and the levy was overruled, but from 1816 until he handed over the administration in 1840, Edmund experienced nothing but ceaseless trouble. Distributing the money available and by the method decreed was bothersome, but extracting the interest from the Commissioners was the main difficulty. He was endlessly writing letters pleading for payment and recommending more profitable forms of investment, and he let it be known that, come what may, the intended beneficiaries in Waterford would not be deprived.

'I am determined never to quit till paid the balance', he wrote in one letter and, in another: 'If anything should happen to this money, in justice I think you would be responsible for it, as it is through your indulgence it would occur.' In an affidavit to the Commissioners he stated: 'I have never received or desired any remuneration whatever for acting as trustee of this charity', and he did his work thoroughly and well. This was attested in 1845, the year after his death, when an accountant, Mr William P. Mathews, audited the account books of the Commissioners. 'I have found that the books of Mr Rice to which I had to refer had been so regularly kept by him since the year 1816 to the present period that I experienced no difficulty in the exercise of my judgment of admitting the several credits claimed upon this evidence solely.'

It is indicative of Edmund Rice's character and the detailed care with which he fulfilled his responsibilities, that such a tribute should have been paid; it is equally indicative that he should have been concerned about saving others from getting entangled in affairs which, as he knew too well from his own experience, could cause them interminable trouble. He was acting with wisdom and kindness when, in 1832, he censured a much-loved friend, Brother Patrick Corbett, Director of the Carrick-on-Suir house. From the goodness of his heart, Brother Patrick had become involved in helping people with problems about wills, property and the like, but Edmund sought to protect him from his own generosity of spirit.

'Your situation as a religious man must be not only dangerous to yourself but productive of scandal to others in the manner in which the greater part of your time is spent about the people of Carrick', he wrote. 'Was it not to avoid having your time engrossed about Mr Ryan's affairs that I prevented you from becoming his executor? And yet you plunge yourself into it in spite of me, even to such a degree that your acts may lug you into difficulties that may not cease to the end of your life. . . . You know there is a rule which forbids Directors to go from home for any length of way without leave from his Superior, and yet you go to Lisentagart, and after to Long Orchard without leave or licence, and by these acts of yours put yourself in much more danger than you were before of becoming accountable to the creditors and legatees of Mr Ryan.'

Having administered this mild rebuke, he directed Brother Patrick to account, at least every fortnight, for every occasion on which he was absent from his monastery for more than half an hour. The purpose of the censure and of the directive were clear, but it took another severe admonition more than a year later to cure the Brother of his well-intentioned habits. He and Edmund Rice remained firm friends, and when a Brother needed a vacation companion, Brother Patrick was invariably the one specially chosen, with expenses paid at the rate of 8/– a week. Three years after he had censured him, Edmund was telling Brother Patrick of yet another law suit in which he himself was unwillingly involved, and through which the Institute could sustain severe losses: 'it is a painful anxiety, but to some of us it is not so much as one may imagine. "The Lord gave, and the Lord taketh away, so blessed be His name for ever and ever". This should be our motto.'

As in every other area of activity, the litigation and the legal matters which punctuated Edmund Rice's life give some insight into his personality. He followed rigid moral principles. As executor or trustee or a party in a court action, he subscribed only to what he considered to be morally right. Everything else took second place, and if there was an advantage to be gained through valid legal means he would not avail of it if it contravened his idea of moral obligation. A good example of his attitude can be seen in respect of a taxation levy for which he was billed in 1838. The firm of solicitors, Messrs Delmege and Ferguson, advised him that he could plead the statute of Limitations and thus avoid paying the debt, but shortly afterwards he replied that he would not evade meeting a fair claim by resorting to a legal device.

He made his will early in 1838 'being weak of body but of sound mind, memory and understanding, thanks to God', and in a brief and simple document left all his assets for the benefit of the Institute and its work. In 1840 he added two codicils to make doubly sure that any debts he may have entered into would be honoured in full. And yet, twenty-three years after he had first come into contact with them, the Commissioners of Charitable Donations and Bequests were causing as much trouble as ever. 'My head is gone to pieces', Edmund wrote in February 1839. 'I am obliged to set off for Dublin this evening. It's well if this work does not kill me.' Another visit to the Commissioners was demanded and Edmund had a nightmarish journey ahead for a man of his age – seventy-seven years. The coach, leaving Waterford at 5 p.m., did not reach Dublin until 11 a.m. next day.

By this time he was no longer Superior General. On 22 February 1838 he went to Mount Sion and started preparations for a special Chapter at which he would resign, and in May he issued a circular to the Brothers which stated: 'Being in a very delicate state of health and quite unable to administer the affairs of the Institute, I deem it expedient to convoke a General Chapter of our Society in July vacation next for the purpose of electing a Superior in my place and discussing such matters as may be deemed expedient for the good of the Society.' A further letter circulated in June contained a typical Rice passage: 'I direct the Brother Director of each house in the Institute to have offered a general Communion and a Mass to get the light of the Holy Ghost on the Chapter, and that on each day from the receipt of this letter till July 24, he have said in common with his community the hymn Veni Creator and the Litany of the Blessed Virgin for the same intention.'

Seventy-six years old and thirty-six years after he had enticed his first reluctant pupils to a converted stable, Edmund had decided that because of his age and physical infirmity, he could no longer cope with the administrative demands of his beloved Institute. The special General Chapter which he summoned met after a preparatory retreat on 24 July 1838, and he presided at the first day's session, which dealt with standing orders and the election of scrutators. Then, briefly and simply, he formally tendered his resignation and moved from the chair which he had occupied as Superior General. The Institute he had founded consisted at the time of seventeen monasteries, forty-three classrooms catering for 7,510 pupils, sixty-two Brothers and six non-teaching Brothers. The average number of pupils per classroom was more than 170 and, in some cases, as high as 250. It was an unsatisfactory situation and while great strides had been made, it was clear that an enormous task remained.

The new Superior General would, in accordance with a request from the 1832 Chapter which Pope Gregory XVI had granted, serve for life rather than ten years, and when the Chapter resumed on 25 July, the man chosen was Brother Michael Paul Riordan, one of the anti-Rice faction from the North Monastery. It was regrettable that his election followed a number of indecisive ballots and a voting procedure that caused controversy.

A native of Clonmel, Brother Riordan was a mature man of forty-nine years. He had had a good education locally, and when he went to Cork in his teens, he secured a job as a clerk in the counting house of a company of silk merchants. He joined Edmund Rice's Institute at the age of thirty-three and was obviously a man of strong personality, much spirituality and considerable talent. He was one of those who helped make the North Monastery an outstanding educational institution, and there can be no doubt that among the Brothers, there was a high regard for his qualities.

It was unfortunate that he assumed the office of Superior General in circumstances that were much less than harmonious. He was elected by nine votes to eight (for Brother Austin Dunphy, a life-long friend and close colleague of Edmund Rice's) and because doubt was cast on the propriety of the voting system, Brother Riordan considered it prudent to submit the facts and a petition to Rome. His election was validated by apostolic authority.

Brother Riordan had been a bitter critic of Edmund Rice's administration and on one particular issue they were in irreconcilable disagreement. From the early days of the Institute, and for reasons which have already been explained, Edmund favoured the introduction of pay-schools as a development which would bring strength, expansion and permanence to the Congregation, but Br Riordan was intransigent in his opposition. The question would continue to cause a great deal of dissension within the Institute until, eventually, the foresight of Edmund Rice would be completely vindicated; but in the late 1830s and early 1840s it came close to creating a disastrous split among the Brothers.

Following his retirement, Edmund played no active part in the controversy, and while his name appeared on two memorials challenging Br Riordan's actions and competence, it was subsequently established that his signature had not been written by him and was probably added without his consent. While Br Riordan may have genuinely felt aggrieved by certain courses of action adopted by Edmund, it should have been altogether clear to him, as it was to so many others of different religions, that everything Edmund had done was inspired by the highest of motives and was carried out in accordance with unimpeachable principles of honesty and morality. Antipathy from the new Superior General, however, remained and, if anything, hardened.

One example occurred when a Chapter was called in 1841 because of the considerable turmoil which existed. At its opening session on 8 July Edmund went to the assembly room thinking, no doubt, that as a former Superior General he was entitled to attend in an ex-officio capacity. A petition to this effect had been sent to the Holy See and an affirmative reply had been received, but because of the vague terms in which the petition had been couched, there was a doubt as to whether a former Superior General could attend all future Chapters or only that at which he had resigned. An opinion had been sought from Father Kenney, and he interpreted the Holy See reply as referring only to the Chapter at which the Superior had resigned.

Obviously unaware of this view, Edmund presented himself and, to the extreme embarrassment of many Brothers, was asked to withdraw while the question of his admission would be discussed. A proposal that he be admitted as an observer was defeated by twelve votes to seven, and so the Founder of the Institute and the man who had dedicated decades of his life to its growth and well-being was debarred from taking part in Chapter deliberations, even as an observer.

Some of those who voted against the proposal were friends of Edmund's and patently felt bound in conscience to adopt this course. In his capacity as Superior General, however, Brother Riordan could have shown a more sensitive approach. He could have used his authority to assuage doubts by recommending that his predecessor should be allowed in with the status of an observer. It must be said in his favour, however, that with the experiences of an uncanonical 1829 Chapter and the questionable aspects of the 1838 Chapter in mind, he was determined to adhere rigidly to the rules.

Just a year earlier Edmund had another humiliating experience during a visit to Dublin. After he retired, he occasionally went to visit old friends, and in June 1840 he made the journey to Limerick where Brother Austin Dunphy was Superior. Some weeks later they both travelled to Dublin on business connected with the North Richmond Street house, and they stayed in Hanover Street, where Brother Bernard Dunphy was Superior. According to the usual custom, they were charged at the rate of 10/– per week for accommodation, but the account books showed an additional charge. The Hanover Street house was in very poor circumstances and no beds were available. Brother Bernard Dunphy applied to North Richmond Street, a community then reduced to two, for the loan of beds but, as he wrote in a letter to Archbishop Murray: 'Out of the many beds they had to spare in the house that Mr. Rice had built and furnished himself, no bed would be given even on loan.'

Brother Dunphy had to go to the remarkable extreme of hiring beds, and the Hanover Street account book recorded: 'To beds borrowed from an upholsterer and to carriage thereof – having been refused the loan of 2 beds in Richmond Street House on two applications although there were many beds vacant there, eight of which and a featherbed belonged to the Hanover Street House – £1–8–0.' There is no record of any reaction from Edmund Rice to this, or to his exclusion from the 1841 Chapter, but it can be assumed that he was grievously hurt, not because of the manner in which he was treated but because of the spirit which was increasingly manifesting itself at the highest levels within the Congregation. It was a spirit which could find no place in his philosophy, and he could not be blamed if he feared that all his years of striving on behalf of the uneducated poor would soon come to nought.

He had made provision in his will and in codicils that all debts contracted by him should be honoured, and there was a discussion on the debts at the 1841 Chapter. Brother Joseph Hearn, who was detailed to audit Edmund's financial affairs, reported: 'No small portion of the debts was caused by expenses incurred in suits to protect the poor, the friendless, the orphan and the widow, or to secure the rights of alms-houses, asylums, or whatever had been left for charitable purposes or pious uses with which he was concerned.' Following the Chapter, it was reported to Archbishop Murray that 'it was resolved that in accordance with the wishes of the late

Superior the debts which he had incurred should be all discharged before the annual proceeds of the general property of the Institute should be applied to any other objects'. This decision was not to Brother Riordan's liking, and in November 1842 he affirmed that 'he had not the slightest intention of taking on himself the onus of liquidating debts contracted by Mr Rice in favour of the Congregation'.

Around the same time, Brother Riordan was complaining to Rome about the conduct of trustees named by Edmund to administer his affairs, and in a letter to Dr Paul Cullen, then Rector of the Irish College, he spoke of the 'few, very few' Brothers who were causing trouble, and once again stated his opposition to pay-schools, the introduction of which 'would be introducing into (the Institute) a mercenary spirit, to the loss of the poor children of this persecuted but faithful country'. He added: 'I do not by any means censure the Ex-Supr. for the part he had taken in these disedifying matters, as he had been labouring under imbecility of mind for some time before he went out of office and has been so ever since. You will please explain this to his Eminence.'

If Brother Riordan believed what he wrote about Edmund Rice's mental state, it makes his attitude of unfriendliness towards a man he considered imbecilic all the more inexplicable, but it is doubtful that he did. He must certainly have been aware of the ample evidence that the Founder was, at the very least, as mentally alert as could be expected from a man of his years. In addition to being sensible enough to recognise that he could no longer perform his duties as Superior General because of his physical health, and to convene a Chapter to accept his resignation, Edmund looked after the charitable affairs entrusted to him as long as he felt himself able to do so efficiently. He was alert enough to give evidence before the Commissioners of Charitable Donations and Bequests, and many perfectly lucid and wise letters were written by him during the period in question. He was also sufficiently sound to recognise the prudence of adding two codicils to his will, and in relation to one particularly dramatic and distressing incident, he displayed a clarity of mind which no moral theologian of his time, or since, could question.

The incident involved another exceptionally painful contretemps between himself and Brother Riordan. It had its origins several years earlier when Mr Bryan Bolger, a man of much wealth and an unqualified admirer of the Institute's work, made available a sum of £1,000 towards the building of the North Richmond Street foundation.

The money was clearly intended as a gift, but this fact was not legally established and, following Mr Bolger's death in 1834, relatives contested his will, which contained substantial bequests to charitable purposes. In the complex legal proceedings that ensued, it was held that the £1,000 given to North Richmond Street was in fact a loan repayable with interest and should thus form part of the deceased man's assets.

This development posed a very serious problem for a poverty-stricken Institute, and it undoubtedly would not have arisen had Mr Bolger foreseen the action his relatives were to take. He would have regularised the donative status of the North Richmond Street contribution but, as matters stood, it appeared that the Institute was indebted to the Bolger estate for the sum involved, plus accrued interest. Edmund Rice and the Brothers connected with him in a trusteeship capacity consulted the firm of solicitors which had been handling the Institute's affairs for years, and all the facts were placed before a senior counsel, Thomas Dickson. On the opinion he submitted, they decided that their obligations could only be met by taking out a mortgage on the North Richmond Street premises.

Brother Riordan placed an incomplete set of facts before a different legal expert, Mr Alexander McCarthy of Cork, and got different advice. Going on the views he had received, he ordered that the mortgage should not be effected 'under the vow of obedience'. Edmund Rice and his colleagues then consulted an eminent Carmelite theologian, Father R. J. Colgan, who held that they would be acting contrary to justice if they did not pursue the course they intended.

Edmund was faced with an agonising dilemma. On the one hand there were his moral probity and the dictates of his conscience and, on the other, there were the authority of his Superior General and his own refined sense of obedience. For a man of his spirituality, the thought of disobeying an order issued under the vow of obedience must have been abhorrent in the extreme: it was, furthermore, an action which could cause grave scandal among members of the Institute not fully conversant with all the facts. Yet there was the indisputable mandate of a sensitive and informed conscience which told him that he must fulfil his moral and legal responsibilities. He acted according to his conscience and a mortgage on North Richmond Street was effected in 1840, but the inner anguish he suffered in the process can only be imagined.

Brother Riordan also obtained the views of a theologian, and they supported the stand he took, but as the theologian based his judgment on legal advice which, in the first instance, was grounded on incomplete facts, it lacked validity. All the circumstances surrounding the mortgage were discussed at the special Chapter in 1841 and, following a report drawn up by a committee on which Brother Riordan served, it was decided that those who had signed the mortgage could not be charged with disobedience because they had acted according to canonical advice, and there was unanimous agreement that the whole sorry business should be buried in oblivion. But not for the first time was Edmund Rice justified in the wisdom, integrity, courage and moral values he applied to actions he felt obliged to take.

In all of this perplexing and hurtful affair, he showed little sign of mental instability, but accusations continued and gained credence. In an undated letter to the Holy See written by Dr Cullen, later to become a distinguished Archbishop of Dublin and Cardinal, there is the astonishing statement: 'When (Mr Rice) became old and stupid, he was dismissed from his charge and resigned it in 1838. For two years after he ceased to be Superior he was not able to understand what he was doing. . . .'

Dr Cullen was undoubtedly influenced by Brother Riordan, and it was extremely sad that a cleric of his importance and influence in Rome should have taken as fact charges of imbecility which were without foundation, and should have been so grossly misinformed as to conclude that Edmund Rice has been 'dismissed' from his post of Superior General.

As we have seen, Edmund voluntarily and responsibly resigned, and during that time when, according to Dr Cullen 'he was not able to understand what he was doing' he was, among other things, resolving with remarkable clear-sightedness an acute conflict of conscience. Only the grave, clearly, would release him from misunderstanding, mis-interpretation and suffering.

15

The Final Days

After he resigned at the 1838 Chapter, Edmund Rice retired into the background. He naturally retained his interest in Institute affairs, but he did not intrude. He was concerned about the policy being pursued, especially in relation to pay schools, and he was unhappily aware of the disharmony which existed. But he did not seek to challenge the authority of the Superior General through the exercise of his personal influence, and he did nothing to exacerbate feelings of antagonism and unrest. He performed his functions as administrator of charitable trusts as long as he felt capable of doing so, and he paid occasional visits to old colleagues in their respective houses. He was always available to give counsel, encouragement and comfort to any Brother or novice who wished to approach him.

Above all else, his last years were concentrated on a deepening of his own spirituality, on a preparation for death. The ultimate inevitability was always in his consciousness. His apostolate was founded on the premise that while education was essential to the attainment of human dignity and fulfilment in this world, it must also be geared to equip people for the infinitely more important life to come. To him, a primary requisite of any worthwhile education was a soul-enriching element: instruction and spirituality were inseparable and in the system which he, an untrained layman, evolved, there was an astonishingly effective balance between the two. Now rid of the vast complexity of activity that had crowded his life, he awaited the approach of the absolute certainty with patient equanimity.

Without the charisma which sprang from his completeness as a human being, he could not have hoped to achieve what he did. Striking leadership qualities were always there and they were recognised and responded to in different ways, by illiterate urchins and by the most influential of dignitaries. They never left him, and the power he had to influence others for their good, particularly spiritually, were with him to the end. Some instances of how he affected people positively in his earlier life have been cited; a later one concerned a Waterford woman named Poll Carthy. She was an inveterate drunkard and, like so many with her affliction, was a terror when she was drunk but kindly and good natured when sober. She had resisted all efforts to reform her until she came under the Rice spell.

Drunkenness was a vicious social evil and, at the time, an understandable one. Alcohol was readily available and inexpensive, and to many it offered the easiest, if not the only, form of release from an intolerably miserable existence. Edmund was aware of the havoc its excessive use could cause in both the material and spiritual senses: so was the Capuchin friar, Father Theobald Mathew who, after several years of localised campaigning, launched his national temperance movement in Cork in 1838 with the words: 'Here goes in the name of the Lord!' Edmund Rice had long been friendly with Father Mathew and a temperance society for juveniles had been established at Mount Sion in 1835 by Brother Joseph Murphy. Its influence throughout Waterford was not inconsiderable and as a result, many travelled to Cork to take the pledge from Father Mathew.

With the purpose of making the trip unnecessary, Bishop Nicholas Foran formed a Waterford branch of the Total Abstinence Society for men in the summer of 1839, and a women's branch followed in November. Father Mathew was invited to address a meeting shortly afterwards, and he arrived unexpectedly on 10 December 'wishing to avoid a popular demonstration'. His first port of call was Mount Sion where 'he was warmly greeted by his dear friend, the venerable Brother Edmund Ignatius Rice'.

Poll Carthy had turned her back on all inducements to join the new movement and her inveterate habit remained unfettered. Then Edmund Rice took an interest in her, and his charisma worked, just as it had worked over the years with prisoners awaiting execution, undisciplined youths and others. Reacting to his approach, Poll agreed to go the Presentation nuns for instruction. She also agreed to take the pledge, but only from the hands of Father Mathew himself, now back in Cork. Having been provided with decent clothes by Edmund, she undertook the journey on foot. She made her promise of sobriety to Father Mathew in person and her penitential pilgrimage – it covered a distance of 150 miles – bore good fruit, for her life was permanently transformed.

Poll probably joined the numerous body of people who held Edmund in reverential admiration. Years later, John Caulfield, The Glen, Waterford, recalled that he was a pupil at Mount Sion during the Founder's lifetime and said: 'I have a distinct recollection of his fatherly kindness as he passed through the classrooms. It would be impossible to exaggerate the reverence and affection members of my family entertained for him because of his many virtues and general pastoral worth. The people of Waterford generally held him in the highest esteem: in fact they idolised the ground he walked on.'

While he was still physically able, Edmund liked to walk in the garden at Mount Sion, and he took immense pleasure in his occasional visits to the classrooms. When the work of the pupils was shown to him, a Brother wrote, he 'generally passed a few words of encouragement and was always thankful for any little service we could do for him'. Brother Stephen Carroll, a native of Dunleer, Co. Louth, who entered the novitiate at North Richmond Street in 1835 and went to Mount Sion three years later, wrote that on calling to Dungarvan, Edmund 'would sit down to hear the boys read – he was particularly fond of their reading. One day as they read through Reeves History of the Bible, when the chapter was finished he made them close their books and asked them on the subject of the lesson. "Why", he asked, "did the Queen procure the death of Nabaoth?". The boys all looked at him and one little fellow said quickly: "Why, sir, to come at the ground!" This answer so quick and rich pleased him, so that he threw himself back in the chair and laughed heartily.'

When he became so weak that he could no longer walk, a wheel-chair was provided, and it enabled him to spend some

time out of doors and to enjoy the panorama of green fields
stretching south from Mount Sion. Young Brothers considered it an honour to be allowed attend on him and one,
Aloysius Hoare, remembered accompanying him on many occasions in the garden. 'Brother, have great devotion to Our
Blessed Lady', Edmund would tell him. 'Say the Memorare in
her honour and she will take care of you and obtain for you
the crowning grace of final perseverance.' In the garden and
in his room he spent almost all of his time saying the Rosary
or reading the Bible or some religious work. When his
eyesight failed, he listened quietly while a Brother read to
him.

Brother Stephen Carroll recorded that he was especially
devout to St Teresa of Avila and greatly attached to her
writings. 'I heard him say', he wrote, 'that he took particular
notice of that saying of hers where she described the poverty
she experienced in one of her foundations, where she says she
had not so much fire in the house as she would roast a sprat
on' Brother Stephen frequently assisted him to retire. 'His
pains were much on the increase and general debility followed. How often would I have heard him say: "Pray, Brother
Stephen, that God's will may be fulfilled in me".'

Brother John Joseph Norris of Carrick-on-Suir entered the
Mount Sion foundation in 1841 and in a memoir recounted
one instance where the wheel-chair was being 'rolled about by
a lay-brother who ran the vehicle very rapidly down a steep
incline and, at the end, turned at right angles and, by upset-
ting the car, pitched (Brother Rice) into a hedge of sharp
thorns, cutting his face and hands. But not a word of complaint escaped his lips, such was his patience. When my turn
came to roll the car, the only observation he made to one of
the Brothers was that he feared I was too flighty, but I took
good care not to go near the incline.'

Edmund was, according to Brother Norris, not only un-
complaining but he was also gentle and, to the end, sensitively
conscious of kindness shown to him. He remained acutely
respectful of authority, for once, when he was very old but yet
capable of walking, however haltingly, 'he took a notion of
visiting the street outside the monastery gate, and though the
servant man endeavoured to prevent him, out he would go.

But when the Superior called him back, he at once, recognising the voice and his own duty to obedience, turned back and never attempted to do it again.'

Edmund could, however, show an odd touch of irritability and impatience, and Brother Carroll experienced one such mild, and regretted, outburst. 'One cold evening', he recalled, 'I came to his room and found him in his chair, and the lay-Brother making up his fire-place. I stood and when he saw me in this position, he said with much displeasure: "Why don't you go and help him make up the fire and not keep looking on?". I was much surprised at his remark and, of course, went to render my humble assistance. But just then all was completed and soon after he retired to his night's rest. Next day when I went to his room, he said to me: "I am very sorry, Brother Stephen, for the manner in which I spoke to you last evening. I am very sorry." I was so confounded at this act of humility that I knew not what to say or think, as I was not in the habit of having such language from such an illustrious individual.'

In December 1841 Edmund became seriously ill, and the Superior General notified the communities about his condition. 'With feelings of pain and sorrow I have to inform you that our very dear Brother Ignatius has been unusually ill. He has no pain or uneasiness, but great weakness which confines him to bed and it is feared will end in his death.' But the end was not yet: Edmund's iron constitution asserted itself and he was, amazingly, again able to attend to personal correspondence. In 1842, however, his mental faculties began to fail and, apart from some lucid periods which grew less frequent, he lived in a state of semi-coma.

A nurse was now in constant attendance – Katie Lloyd, sister of Brother John Lloyd – and prayer had become such an integral part of Edmund's life that his first words on awaking each morning were, she reported, 'Praise be to you, O Christ', even though he did not appear to know what he was saying. In August 1844, his general condition deteriorated rapidly, and in addition to members of the community who were constantly at his bedside, Bishop Foran paid several visits. It was known throughout Waterford that the end was near for one whom many considered a 'walking saint'.

Brother Stanislaus Hyland, who was preparing for his profession, recorded that on 28 August 'I had just returned from St. Patrick's branch schools, and I at once ran up to see him. He clasped my hand in his, now clammy before death. I noticed his grasp growing unconsciously closer and a doze seemed to come on him. His eyes were glassy. I was expecting the bell to ring for dinner and I said aloud to him: "Good-bye, sir, the bell will soon ring." I disengaged my hand from his grasp and he awoke and said to me: "Good-bye and God bless you, my child." Mine was the last hand, I think, he shook in friendship on this earth.' Brother Hyland was right in his reference to the clamminess of death, but not in assuming that the last hand-shake had been given.

Shortly after 4 a.m. next morning, the nurse rang the bell to call the Brothers to the bedside, for Edmund had suffered an apoplectic fit and his breathing had become markedly heavier. The Mount Sion community assembled and soon the room in which their beloved Founder lay dying was crowded. As the nurse was leaving, Edmund called to her. He 'thanked her for what she had done for him by shaking hands with her and blessing her'. His last wish was typical: it was 'that she and her family should never want, and that the Brothers would be good to her and all of them'. He died peacefully shortly after 11 a.m.

Dressed in the habit of the Institute, a crucifix and Rosary entwined in his hands, his body was placed in the small oratory of the monastery, and as Brothers maintained a vigil, the Mayor of Waterford, many of the city's leading citizens and scores of past pupils came to pay their respects. The news spread rapidly and *The Waterford Mail* reported that 'this venerable man . . . had borne his protracted illness with patience and resignation to the Divine will. . . . He was a man of indefatigable zeal and charity, endowed with great prudence, energy and perseverance.'

The Tipperary Vindicator referred to him as 'a venerable, a good and, in the best sense of the word, a great man – a man of powerful mind, of vast knowledge and human nature, of a comprehensive grasp of intellect, of undaunted courage, of irresistible perseverance, of unbending integrity, of pure piety, of immense charity . . . the herald of a new age of Irishmen in the way of instruction, the harbinger of virtue and of blessings'.

On 31 August Bishop Foran and twenty-nine priests attended the funeral obsequies and Edmund Rice was laid to rest in the north-east corner of the small monastery cemetery which was consecrated that same day. A plain stone cross was erected to mark the place. It carried the simple inscription

BROTHER EDMUND IGNATIUS RICE:
DIED AUGUST 29, 1844:
FOUNDER OF THE CONGREGATION OF
THE BROTHERS OF THE
CHRISTIAN SCHOOLS OF IRELAND.

Back in 1802 when Edmund Rice converted a stable in New Street into a crude classroom, a Quaker friend voiced his misgivings. Another Quaker was present at the funeral in Mount Sion and he wrote later to a Protestant friend: 'The display of feeling manifested at the interment of Brother Rice shows that the people are neither forgetful not ungrateful. No wonder, as they see the extraordinary change in the face of the country brought about mainly by his instrumentality. The Roman Catholics believe he was a messenger from God. I knew Mr Rice well. I respected his nobleness of character. I can appreciate the work he has accomplished.

'Who could stand by his grave and witness unmoved the wave of sorrow of the vast multitude? Seeing it, I was almost moved to cry out: "Why are you sorrowful? Why are you sad?" Mr Rice is not dead. Yes, he lives – the highest, noblest and greatest life. He lives in the noble band of Christian workmen to whom he has bequeathed his spirit and his work.'

16

'He is not Dead'

In their respective ways, three men made a profound impact
on the Irish scene during the early part of the nineteenth century. Daniel O'Connell was a colossus – a brilliant orator, an
outstanding lawyer, a pacifist political agitator of formidable
power, and a leader of magnetic appeal who was hated by sections of the English ascendancy with a ferocity only matched
by the extent of the hero-worship accorded to him by the mass
of his own people. He was criticised for his attitude towards
the Irish language, but to the vast majority, he was their
champion, their emancipator, their liberator and their hope.

Father Theobald Mathew became a national figure when
he launched his remarkable temperance movement. His campaign against the widespread and insidious evil of alcohol
abuse swept the country with dramatic success, and as the
zealous Capuchin tirelessly preached, exhorted and cajoled,
every open-air rally he addressed attracted huge numbers and
every church in which he spoke was full to overflowing. The
temperance crusade made palpable common sense, and with
the public imagination fired by the sanctity and sincerity of
the initiator, Father Mathew rivalled the great O'Connell in
the affection and admiration of the Irish.

Edmund Rice was the third outstanding influence of the
period and, perhaps, the most important. There were many
parts of the country in which his name was unknown, and
there were substantial sections of the community unaware of
his existence or of his Institute. The nature of the activities in
which they were involved demanded maximum public exposure on the parts of O'Connell and Father Mathew: such a
demand was not made on Edmund Rice in his apostolate, and
had it been made, his retiring disposition would certainly

have shrunk from it, but in his own vitally important area, he quietly strove and doggedly persevered, and it was only in decades and generations to come that the full extent of his immense achievement would be recognised throughout Ireland and in many regions all over the world.

'In times to come, people will not give me due credit for the winning of Catholic Emancipation', O'Connell wrote, 'for it will not enter into the mind of man to conceive of what race of slaves I have to endeavour to make men.' Edmund Rice expressed no concern as to what future opinion of his role would be; he was content to do his utmost and pray that God's will would be fulfilled in him. But his role was closely complementary to those of the two other giant figures of his time, and particularly to that of O'Connell, who more than once paid signal tribute to the part being played by the Christian Brothers in making men of slaves.

The death of Edmund Rice caused much deep sorrow, and it was expressed with poignant simplicity by those who were most dear to his heart. Leading dignitaries paid their tributes, but so also did the humble and unknown, like John Flynn of Waterford. 'I went to school to Brother Rice', he said, 'and he was a grand man who was pious, holy and charitable. He was very affectionate and kind to the children. Rich and poor were equally dear to him. When leaving school the boys shook hands with him, and next morning if they had been beaten by their parents, they would show him the place to make it well.'

In Dublin, Anne McDonnell had much the same to say when she recalled: 'My eldest son was under the instruction of Brother Rice. He was stopping from school one time and I brought him to Brother Rice and asked him to punish the lad. Brother Rice said that it was against the rules of the school for him to punish the boy and that I should do the punishing myself. "Wait until I catch him home and won't I punish him!" said I. Brother Rice laughed heartily at my boasting and he took the boy from me. He told me not to be hard on him. . . . Brother Rice was kindness itself to the boys and he was one of the mildest of men. He was mild in manner and mild in appearance. The people loved him and thought him a saint.'

John Flynn and Anne McDonnell were representative of

countless others; and because relatively few of the throng
which turned up for the funeral on 31 August could attend the
Requiem Mass or witness the interment in the Mount Sion
cemetery, Bishop Foran announced that a Month's Mind
would be held in the Cathedral on 1 October. It was an
astonishing demonstration of love and reverence. Dr Foran
presided at the Mass; the Mayor and Aldermen of Waterford,
Catholic and Protestant, attended in their ceremonial robes;
Father Mathew made the journey from Cork; hundreds of
pupils from Mount Sion and the Presentation convent
marched to the Cathedral, which had no seating. Many had
to stay in the street outside. 'Never was such a scene in our
Cathedral as was presented yesterday', *The Waterford Chronicle*
reported next day.

In a panegyric, Father Richard Fitzgerald, confessor to
Mount Sion for many years, said it would be impossible 'to
exaggerate the blessings that have accrued to society through
the agency of the education establishments that have been
reared by Edmund Rice's piety, his energy and his zeal. . . .
For as long as religion shall be reverenced among us; for as
long as civilisation shall be prized and cherished; for as long
as exalted patriotism shall be accounted a virtue, the name of
Edmund Rice will be held in benediction.'

Edmund Rice was at rest in a tranquil corner of Mount
Sion, his duty done, his tribulations over. Yet he lived. In
mid-October, Bishop Foran presided at a meeting which
resolved to open a public subscription so that a memorial in
his honour might be erected. It would take the form of an extension to Mount Sion consisting of a classroom and chapel.
No more fitting memorial could be imagined. Together, classroom and chapel symbolised in a peculiarly sensitive way
everything Edmund had stood for and worked for over more
than forty years of heroic endeavour.

The foundation stone of the extension was laid on 8
September 1845, and one of those present was Thomas
Francis Meagher, 'Meagher of the Sword', the man whose
subsequent colourful life of political agitation, deportation, escape and adventure would end in mystery while he was acting
Governor of the U.S. state of Montana. 'While I stood a silent
witness of that scene', he wrote, 'I was almost prompted to ex-

claim: "Friends, mourners and admirers of a great man, your work is needless! The good, wise and venerable man, Edmund Rice, to whom you this day raise a monument, has anticipated your gratitude and has reared with his own strong hands a monument that mankind shall reverence and heaven shall bless. There is not a soul instructed, ennobled, purified in these schools of which he has been the founder that will not be his monument which neither the rust nor the moth shall consume."'

Brother Joseph Murphy had been an outspoken critic of Edmund during the days of acrimony but now, as Superior of Mount Sion, he was conscious of more important things than administrative or policy conflicts. 'His death was a greater affliction to me than I had expected', he wrote. 'You may suppose what I must have felt at seeing so great and good a man expire – one with whom I was so intimately connected for nearly forty years by the ties of religion and friendship. His life was a long series of sufferings, labours and contradictions under which he manifested a greatness of soul which betokened sublime virtue. . . . Solid piety, rare prudence, ardent zeal and great love of the poor and afflicted seemed to shape the character of his virtues.'

The Mount Sion classroom and chapel took shape and reached completion. The chapel was solemnly blessed by Bishop Foran on 4 April 1846, and the high altar, donated by the communities in England, was granted the honour Altare Privilegiatum by Pope Pius IX. The new classroom was quickly filled and Edmund's first foundation proceeded with its work, even though the problems of making ends meet remained, and would remain for years to come. The Great Hunger was at hand.

With the passage of time, the name of Edmund Rice was not forgotten; rather it grew in honour and esteem, and his reputation for sanctity increased in the public consciousness. James Holden of Callan remembered that his father knew Edmund well and Edmund 'used frequently be referred to in fireside conversation as "Saint Ignatius Rice". When on occasion someone might query the term "saint", he would be told: "If he is not a saint he deserves to be canonised."' Mary Morrissey of Waterford also recounted: 'We have in this house

four cups and saucers which my grandfather won in Mount
Sion while a pupil there, Brother Rice held some kind of raffle
and presented these cups with his own hand. There were six
in the set, but two cups and saucers were broken. We treasure
these cups most carefully. My mother would never allow them
to be used.' Brother Michael Xavier Weston of Waterford
wrote: 'I have frequently invoked Brother Rice's intercession,
and never without having benefitted by my doing so. When in
very ill health in Waterford, suffering from extreme weakness
and spitting of blood, I asked him as I knelt at his grave to obtain from God that I might gain strength enough at least to
continue my work in the schools. My request was granted: the
blood-spitting ceased and I have ever since been able to carry
on my work.'

On 28 June 1871, the remains of Edmund Rice were
privately removed from their original resting place and
transferred to the centre of the Mount Sion cemetery's north
side, and in 1940 it was decided to build a special mausoleum
after the manner of a Gothic chapel in which the remains of
the Founder and of all the others buried in the little cemetery
would be placed. The disinterment of the Founder took place
on 15 July in the presence of Bishop Jeremiah Kinane, and as
the mausoleum was not yet ready, the bones were temporarily
deposited in the foundation's sacristy.

On 14 May 1941, the remains were taken to the parish
church of Trinity Without, Ballybricken, where they
remained overnight on a catafalque in front of the high altar,
and following Requiem Mass next day, the funeral procession
to Mount Sion passed the site of the first Rice school in New
Street – the impossibly modest starting point of a movement
which had, by now, become world-wide. It says something for
the enduring love and admiration on the part of the people
that, almost a century after Edmund's death, thousands lined
the streets, filed past the coffin and attended the church
ceremonies. Edmund still lived.

Yet one more journey remained, short and final. On 26
August 1979 a new Chapel of the Blessed Sacrament was
dedicated at Mount Sion and, after an open-air Mass, the
casket containing Edmund's remains was carried to its last,
honoured resting place beneath a stained-glass rose window

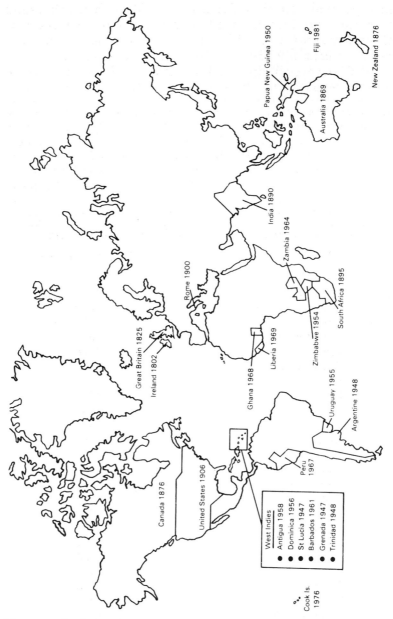

The spread of the Christian Brothers and the Presentation Brothers throughout the world.

incorporated from the old mausoleum. More than a thousand Christian Brothers from all over the world were present; Church and State joined in impressive tribute and, as always, public interest was displayed by huge throngs of people.

Of all the events connected with Edmund Rice, this was the most splendid. The Papal Nuncio in Ireland, Dr Gaetano

---

Edmund Rice set up his first school for poor boys in a stable at New Street, Waterford, in 1802. From that humble beginning his mission has spread, through the labours of the Brothers he founded, to twenty-five countries. His Brothers, now numbering 3,000, working with 7,000 other teachers, instruct over 212,000 boys in 560 schools. They conduct orphanages and schools for the poor, primary and second level schools, university colleges, schools for the deaf and for the blind, technical schools and agricultural colleges.

C = Christian Brothers   P = Presentation Brothers

		Country	Foundation Date
C	P	Ireland	1802
C	P	Great Britain	1825
C		Australia	1869
C	P	Canada	1876
C		New Zealand	1876
C		India	1890
C		South Africa	1895
C		Rome	1900
C	P	U.S.A.	1906
	P	Grenada	1947
	P	St Lucia	1947
C		Argentina	1948
	P	Trinidad	1948
C		Papua New Guinea	1950
C		Zimbabwe	1954
C		Uruguay	1955
C		Dominica	1956
C		Antigua	1958
	P	Barbados	1961
C		Zambia	1964
C	P	Peru	1967
	P	Ghana	1968
C		Liberia	1969
C		Cook Islands	1976
C		Fiji Islands	1981

Alibrandi, was there, and so was the Cardinal Archbishop of Armagh, Dr Tomas O Fiaich. The State was represented at the highest level by President Patrick Hillery, and the Cardinal Archbishop of Los Angeles, Dr Timothy Manning, preached a homily. In recognition of the occasion, the City of Waterford paid its homage to Edmund Rice and all of those who had served his apostolate down the years by conferring its Freedom on Very Rev. G. G. McHugh, Superior General of the Christian Brothers. From Rome, Pope John Paul II sent his blessing and his hope 'that the life and work of the Founder of the Christian Brothers will be an ever more powerful inspiration to those who have accepted God's call to the honour of serving Him in that Congregation'.

In his homily, Cardinal Manning asked for prayers that the cause for Edmund Rice's canonisation might prosper. He was, he said, a man of heroic sanctity, a man of great consequence for his times and also a man for our times. 'We feel', the Cardinal added, 'that the re cognition at this time of the life and apostolate of Edmund Rice is an alerting to parents, teachers and peers of the need for true Gospel values in education, for the integration of religion with life issues, for the permeation of the secular world with the perspective of the city of God and, that in the ultimate plan of God, all creation and the works of man will be transformed to glory.'

The cause for canonisation was introduced by the decision of a General Chapter of the Christian Brothers in 1910, and an Historical Commission was established by Dr John Charles McQuaid, Archbishop of Dublin, in 1961. A large mass of documents has been presented to the Sacred Congregation for the Causes of Saints in Rome, and in it are innumerable examples of the subject's reputation for exceptional sanctity. At the dedication of the Chapel of the Blessed Sacrament, Brother McHugh also referred to the cause of canonisation: 'It is our earnest desire and prayer that if it be for God's glory and the sanctification of souls, the holiness of Edmund Rice will soon be formally sanctioned by the Church', he said.

Brother McHugh also referred to the cause for canonisation: 'It is our earnest desire and prayer that, if it be for God's glory and the sanctification of souls, the holiness of

Edmund Rice will soon be formally sanctioned by the Church', he said. He added that 'it is because we are concerned about Christ's mission in the world now and in the future that we wish to see Edmund Rice presented to the world as an example and a source of hope'. In the infant days of the nineteenth century Edmund showed an example and became a source of rich and positive hope. Towards the end of the twentieth century, the problems may be different, but the need for example and hope is greater than ever. Edmund Rice was, according to several opinions, someone raised up by God to serve a particular purpose at a particular time. But he was also a man for all time, at once contemplative and a man of action, a visionary and a realist, a person who could blend to the ultimate degree a mystical love of God with a practical love of humanity. Such a type comes seldom.

Edmund still lives. The many pilgrims who visit the place of his birth near Callan and the Chapel of the Blessed Sacrament at Mount Sion are among those who feel his presence. They would agree with the Quaker who wrote: 'He lives, yes, he lives – the highest, noblest and greatest life. He lives in the noble band of Christian workmen to whom he has bequeathed his spirit and his work.'

Cause for Canonisation

At the time of his death Edmund Rice had an extraordinary reputation for sanctity, particularly among the ordinary people, not only in Waterford but also in centres like Dungarvan and Dublin and, indeed, in places where schools had been established by the Christian Brothers but had not been visited by their founder. The esteem accorded him was not confined to those in the adult age group. Patrick Brown of Waterford, who was a pupil at Mount Sion from 1837 and had a personal knowledge of Edmund, recalled: 'Boys had so much veneration for Brother Rice that they regarded it as a privilege even to get a look at him'. Over and over again in testimony submitted from many parts of the country the same words and phrases keep cropping up: holy, pious, loving, saintly, charitable, kind, a man raised by God, a good and great man. John Caulfield, a pupil at Mount Sion in Edmund's time said it 'would be impossible to exaggerate the esteem, affection and reverence' people entertained for Edmund and added: 'In fact they idolised the ground he walked on'. That the esteem was shared by the Brothers was made clear by Margaret Doheny in 1912. She had been living in the old Rice home at Westcourt and she testified that Christian Brothers often called to see the room in which Edmund first saw the light of day. 'They sometimes kissed the walls of the room out of respect for the holy man who was born in it', she said.

Yet because of policies followed by his successors, Edmund faded into the background as far as the Brothers were concerned and it was not until 1911 that the first attempt was made to introduce the cause for his canonisation. The initiative came from Brother Calasanctius Whitty, the then

Superior General. He commissioned Brother Mark Hill to collect testimonies, but the work came to an abrupt halt when a document discovered in Rome was considered an insuperable barrier to the Cause. However the document was subsequently proved to be a forgery. Interestingly it was Cardinal Montini, the future Pope Paul VI, who was responsible for a resumption of operations relating to the cause. He was being taught English by Brother Alexis Clarke, then Procurator at the Brothers' Generalate in Rome, and he showed a keen interest in the founder of a Congregation which had become worldwide and which held a place of honour and distinction in the heart of Christendom. The forged document, Cardinal Montini assured Brother Alexis, would not be an obstacle, and in due course a letter was obtained from the Holy Office stating that there was no objection to the cause proceeding.

The cause was officially opened in the Archdiocese of Dublin in 1957 with the establishment of an Historical Commission. However, progress was extremely slow and an irritating problem materialised in 1968 when a General Chapter of the Congregation in Melbourne received a statement from the Chancellor of the Archdiocese declaring that because of difficulties which had arisen in the documentation the Historical Commission had reached a negative decision. For a second time the cause had stalled but, nothing daunted, the Brothers at the Melbourne Chapter were convinced that objections arising out of the documentation, and relating to the validity of signatures on compromising material, could be successfully refuted. They decided, therefore, to appeal, and their action was endorsed by the Holy See: it ruled, in 1969, that the Dublin Historical Commission had exceeded its brief. A second Commission was appointed and, thanks to the tireless and committed work of its secretary, Father Kevin Kennedy, a fresh start led to a favourable report in 1976. Two years later Monsignor Sean O'Kelly was appointed Postulator of the Cause and, when he died, he was succeeded by Father Dermot Cox, O.F.M.

The *Positio*, an official statement on Edmund's life, work and virtues running to more than 1,200 pages, was prepared and examined by six historical consultors of the

Congregation of Saints and their individual evaluations, presented in 1989, were unanimously positive. In the next significant development, nine theological consultors were also unanimous in finding that Edmund had led a life of heroic virtue and, with the historical and theological consultors unanimous in their conclusions, Pope John Paul II declared Edmund Rice Venerable. The ceremony took place in the Consistorial Hall at the Vatican on Friday, 2 April, 1993. Meanwhile, a Miracle Tribunal set up in Ireland in 1988 was carrying out an intensive investigation into a miracle attributed to Edmund's intercession. The tribunal was organised by Brother Stan Carroll of St Mary's Province, Ireland. Documentation relating to the cure involved had been collected by Brother Columba Normoyle and a key person in the proceedings was the tribunal's notary, Monsignor John Hanly, former Rector of the Irish College, Rome, and the person mainly responsible for the canonisation of St Oliver Plunkett. The tribunal started work in March 1988, and evidence under oath, running to 329 pages, was taken from fourteen witnesses. In addition to Catholics, they included members of the Church of Ireland, Presbyterian, Baptist and Methodist churches.

It is not surprising that Edmund Rice's extraordinary reputation for sanctity should have speedily generated a devotion to him. From the moment of his death his intercession was sought, and countless favours and cures have been attributed to him. One Brother who became a member of the Congregation at Mount Sion in 1893, Michael Xavier Weston, recorded that he frequently invoked Edmund's intercession and never without having benefited from doing so. In recent times, accounts have come from many parts of the world and embrace a wide diversity of content. So a woman in Claremorris, Co. Mayo, Ireland, gave Edmund the credit for finding a lost wedding ring, as did a student in Rondebosch, South Africa, for passing an examination. In more serious cases, cures have been attributed to him of milliary tuberculosis (Papua New Guinea), of bowel cancer (Indooroopilly, Australia), of cancer in a man who had been given two months to live (Baldoyle, Co. Dublin), and of a boy with peritonitis (Geraldton, West Australia). In this case the surgeon who operated on the boy could not remove the appendix because of its abscessed state, and he advised the Superior of the Brothers' school, where the boy was a student, that there was no hope. The condition deteriorated when a second medical intervention revealed that other abscesses had formed. But after a relic of Edmund Rice had been placed under the patient's pillow and prayers had been said, a third medical intervention showed that the abscesses were drying up.

There were several options available in advancing Edmund's cause from the stage of Venerable to that of Blessed. An authenticated miracle was necessary for beatification, and three inexplicable cures were to hand. In one, a Dominican priest was suffering from jaundice so severe that his liver and kidneys had ceased to function and the surgeon in charge said: 'Whether I operate on this man or not, he will die'. The Prior and community of the priest's Abbey were notified of his impending death and the Prior had taken out his habit to lay him out. For many years the patient had offered devotion to Edmund Rice and he treasured a framed portrait of Edmund which had been presented to him by someone in Callan. As he lay on what was presumed to be his death bed in a Dublin hospital, he asked those around him to pray to Edmund and requested that the beloved portrait be brought to him. Before long he had 'made a most remarkable recovery which, to some extent, was unexplained under the circumstances'.

A second likely case concerned a farmer who had his gall-stones removed. During the operation a large mass assumed to be cancer of the lower bile duct or adjacent pancreas was discovered and was considered to be inoperable, but a by-pass procedure was carried out between the common bile duct and the duodenum for symptomatic relief. The diagnosis of cancer was never clinically established as no biopsy was carried out, but the doctor in charge reported that the patient's complaint was inoperable and that his condition was 'quite hopeless'. Actually the patient was screened off to die. A prayer for the Confirmation of the Virtue of Edmund Rice was sent by a Christian Brother to the farmer and, after reading the prayer, he fell into a coma and couldn't see. Next day, however, he could see perfectly: he said the prayer many times and his recovery was quick and remarkable. 'It was he who cured me', he said later, referring to Edmund Rice. The prayer runs: 'O God, who in Thy love for the souls of innocent children, didst choose Edmund Rice to establish a new family in Thy Church for their instruction, look favourably, I beseech Thee, on his virtues and good works, and if it be for Thy glory and the sanctification of souls, mercifully hear my prayer that he may be raised to the altars of Thy Holy Church. Amen'.

The case eventually chosen for putting before the medical board of the Congregation of Saints concerned a nineteen-year-old boy who was admitted to hospital suffering from severe abdominal pain and vomiting a considerable amount of blood. A tentative diagnosis suggested a perforated ulcer, but a laparotomy (opening of the abdomen) revealed a volvulus, a twisting of the intestine causing an internal obstruction which would explain the symptoms of extreme pain and anaemia due to loss of blood. Indeed the symptoms were so severe that, in the words of one medical expert, 'they indicated a major abdominal catastrophe'. The boy's condition worsened so much his mother felt matters were hopeless 'and prayed that God would take him'. Some days later, after a second laparotomy had been carried out, the unanimous medical opinion was that the youth had no more than forty-eight hours to live.

In the first laparotomy, the affected bowel was treated with the application of hot saline packs and, because it showed signs of recovery after an hour, the abdomen was closed. The patient's condition subsequently deteriorated, however, and a second laparotomy was carried out. During it the medical team tried to locate healthy bowel which could be used to allow the digestive system to function, but they found nothing but gangrenous bowel. The operation lasted considerably more than two hours, and the most ominous aspect was that the senior surgeon, two assistant surgeons and two anaesthetists could not, between them, find any viable bowel. A suggestion was made that the boy be moved to another hospital which had more sophisticated equipment, but the senior surgeon felt that there was no point in the transfer because there was nothing in the patient to operate on: the case was hopeless. The next day the youth was given the last rites of the Catholic Church and a priest talked to him of suffering and death, explained to him that he was dying. The parents informed friends of the position by telephone and discussed funeral arrangements. Before she left the hospital to return home, the mother in fact thought her son was already dead and 'was thankful to God that his suffering was over'. The patient himself recalled: 'I was quite aware that death was, more or less, imminent for me... I wasn't frightened, because I had been through a lot of suffering'. He mentioned that on the days following the second laparotomy: 'The pain was very severe – in fact it was so severe I could nearly bend the bars of the bed. I was in agony'.

As is the tradition in the hospital relative to terminally ill patients with little time left, instructions were issued that the boy was to be made as comfortable as possible, that he was to be treated with large doses of painkilling morphine (it was given through a vein because he was too thin to receive a muscular injection) and that he was to be allowed indulge his whims in respect of food – when he expressed a wish for a ham sandwich, for instance, it was provided, and he was also given some scrambled egg and ice-cream. But the expected fatal deterioration didn't take place and a very remarkable development was noticed by a nurse two days after the second laparotomy – at a time when, according to the prognosis, the youth should have been dead.

The patient had had a light diet of scrambled egg and the nurse was later astonished when she noticed digested food coming out of the faecal fistula, the artificially-made opening for the release of body waste. She could not understand how this could happen because bowel functions had been nil: actually with no viable bowel, functions couldn't have been otherwise than nil, and the fact of digested food coming through was inexplicable. In any event, the patient was still alive. Two days later he was transferred to the hospital with more sophisticated equipment where a third laparotomy was performed. The youth was anaesthetised, but before the abdomen was opened the theatre nurse 'pulled out literally feet of dead bowel, which had actually been sticking out through the abdominal wall'. When the abdomen was opened the surgeon underwent an experience he had never had before. There was nothing to find: the abdominal cavity was empty because it was just a granulation cavity. There was no sign of any organs, any bowel or anything. But on dissection into the area of the duodeno-jejunal flexure, some viable small bowel was found, and it was possible to release, and join together with a circular stapling gun, about thirty centimetres of the upper small bowel and about forty centimetres of the lower. When this procedure was completed, the patient turned the corner and improved dramatically.

On the evening of the second laparotomy, a Brother in the local Christian Brothers school had heard of the youth's impending death and hastened to the parents' house with a relic of Edmund Rice. The relic was taken to the hospital and placed under the patient's pillow, and parents, relatives, friends and neighbours concentrated their intercessionary prayers on Edmund. Within forty-eight hours of five medical experts failing to find viable bowel in an operation lasting more than two hours, food was being digested through viable bowel. Taking this and all other relevant facts into consideration, the medical tribunal of the Congregation of Saints unanimously found that the recovery of the patient was inexplicable by natural means. The patient himself told members of the miracle tribunal in Ireland: 'I attribute the fact that I'm sitting here before you now to the relic', and his parents had no doubt that his life had been spared through the intercession of Edmund Rice.

Another miracle, accepted by the medical tribunal, definitely attributable to Edmund and worked after the official beatification declaration, will need to occur before the cause can proceed to the final stage of canonisation. The time scale and nature of events cannot be anticipated or speculated upon, but there will be no scarcity of people eager and willing to pray that the Church will give official endorsement to the opinion of those people in Waterford, Callan, Dublin and elsewhere who, in mourning Edmund's death in 1844, talked of 'a good and great man', 'a man sent from God' and 'a walking saint'.

Index

162 *Edmund Rice: The Man and His Times*

Finn, Br Patrick, 37
Fitzgerald, Rev. Richard, 147
Fitzgerald, W. J., 87
FitzGibbon, Attorney General, 7
Flannery, Rev. Thomas, 79
Fleming, Bishop Michael Anthony, 98
Flood, Henry, 12
Flynn, John, 146
Fontana, Cardinal, 71-2
Foran, Bishop Nicholas, 139, 142, 144, 147, 148
Franzoni, Cardinal, 94

George III, 29
George IV, 106
Gibraltar, 64, 99 et seq.
Gould, Sir George, 74
Grace, Br John Austin, 77
Grace, Rev. Patrick, 12
Grattan, Henry, 77
Gregory XVI, Pope, 130
Grosvenor, Br Thomas, 37

Hall, Mr and Mrs S. C., 44
Halley, Br Philip, 64-5
Hanly, Mons. John, 156
Harrington, Wilfred O.P., ix
Hearn, Francis, 51
Hearn, Br Joseph, 133
Hearn, Dean T., 38, 41, 51
Hibernian Society, Schools of, 33
Hill, Br Mark, 155
Hillery, President Patrick, 152
Hoare, Br Aloysius, 141
Hogan, William, 58
Holden, James, 148
Holmes, Robert, 108
Howley, Rev. William, 80
Hughes, Rev. Henry, 103
Hussey, Bishop T., 32, 38, 40, 41, 66
Hyland, Rev. R. H., 55
Hyland, Br Stanislaus, 143

Inglis, H. D., 10, 54, 58

James I, 5
James II, 6
John Paul II, Pope, 152, 156

Kearney, Rev. Philip, 96
Kee, Robert, 13
Kelly, Br Myles, 123
Kelly, Bishop Patrick, 86 et seq.
Kenney, Rev. Peter, 75, 78, 116, 132
Kildare Place Society, 93, 110

Kinane, Bishop Jeremiah, 149

Lanigan, Bishop J., 35
Lansdowne, Marquis of, 107
Lecky, W. E. H., 5
Leinster, Duke of, 108
Leo XII, Pope, 90
Leonard, Br John, 60, 118, 124
Leonard, Br Patrick Joseph, 60, 115, 116, 117, 118, 119, 121, 122, 123, 124
Limerick, 62, 63, 65
Liverpool, 97
Lloyd, Katie, 142
London, 64, 96, 97

McCarthy, Alexander, 135
McDermott, Br Ignatius, 60
McDonnell, Anne, 146
McEnroe, Rev. J., 98
MacGearailt, Piaras, 12
McHale, Archbishop John, 108, 113
McHugh, Br G. G., 152
Madgett, Bishop Nicholas, 14
Manchester, 64, 96
Manifold, Br Francis, 63
Manning, Timothy Cardinal, 152
Marum, Bishop Kieran, 16, 80
Mathew, Rev. Theobald, 139, 145, 147
Mathews, William P., 128
Meagher, Thomas Francis, 147
Miracles, 156-60
Miracle Tribunal, 156
Montini, Cardinal, 155
Moretti, Girolamo, 71
Morrissey, Mary, 148
Moylan, Bishop F., 59, 78
Mountjoy, Viscount, 105
Mulcahy, Br James, 58, 81
Mulcahy, Br John, 40, 58, 59
Murphy, Joan, 24, 35
Murphy, Bishop John, 68, 73, 74, 75, 77
Murphy, Br Joseph, 96, 139, 148
Murphy, Br Patrick, 89
Murray, Bishop, later Archbishop, Daniel, 61, 68, 72, 74, 92, 93, 94, 98, 99, 102, 104, 108, 112, 113
Murray, John F., 109

Nagle, Nano, 33, 59
National System of Education, 93, 104 et seq.
Newbury, Earl of, 97
Newport, Sir John, M.P., 46, 55

Norfolk, Duke of, 97
Normoyle, Br Columba, xi, 156
Norris, Br John Joseph, 141

O'Connell, Daniel, 103, 105, 106, 107, 108, 125, 145, 146
O'Connor, Br Jerome, 59
O'Donnell, Rev. Patrick Louis, 22
O Fiaich, Tomas Cardinal, 152
O'Flaherty, Br Patrick, 99, 100, 101
O'Meagher, Rev. Patrick, 70, 79 et seq.
Ormond, Duke of, 8
O Suilleabhain, Amhlaoibh, 10, 17
O'Sullivan, Tadhg Gaelach, 29

Paul VI, Pope, 155
Peel, Sir Robert, 36, 106
Phelan, Br Francis, 64
Pietro, Cardinal, 67
Pius VI, Pope, 32, 35, 66
Pius VII, Pope, 66, 72, 74, 85
Pius IX, Pope, 148
Plunkett, St Oliver, 14, 156
Positio, 155-6
Power, Rev., later Bishop, John, 33, 41, 47, 58, 66, 67, 68, 78, 126
Power, Patrick Canon, 80
Power, Rev. Pierce, 80
Power, Mary, 125
Presentation Brothers, 74
Presentation Sisters, 31, 33, 59, 67, 81, 89, 114
Preston, 64, 96

Rice, Edmund, born, 2; early education, 15, secondary education, 18; businessman, 21; marriage, 24; establishes first school, 35 et seq.; founds Mount Sion, 38; first vows, 47; accused in forged letters, 69 et seq.; granted Papal Brief, 72; appointed first Superior General, 75; attitude to pay-schools, 86 et seq.; attitude to National system of Education, 107 et seq.; transfers to North Richmond St, Dublin, 105; resigns as Superior General, 130; charged with mental incapacity, 115, 116, 134; death, 143
Rice, John, 51
Rice, Rev. John, 13, 37, 100
Rice, Sister Josephine, 16, 24

Rice, Mary, 24
Rice, Margaret, 16
Rice, Maurice, 18
Rice, Michael, 18, 22
Rice, Patrick, 2
Rice, Robert, 2, 3
Riordan, Br Michael Austin, 74
Riordan, Br Michael Paul, 91, 92, 94, 118, 121, 124, 130, 132, 134
Royal Schools, 33
Ryan, Br Jerome Francis, 60, 94
Ryan, Br Roger, 89

Sadlier, Dr, 108
Sheehy, Rev. Nicholas, 14
Shiel, Lalor, 125
Shrewsbury, Earl of, 97
Sisters of Charity, 73
Smith, Charles, 21, 23
Stanley, E. G., 108
Sughrue, Bishop Charles, 79
Sunderland, 96
Surrey, Earl of, 97
Swift, Jonathan, 7

Tierney, Margaret, 3
Tighe, William, 9, 16
Thurles, 62, 65, 72
Troy, Bishop, later Archbishop, John, 15, 61, 68, 71

Wakefield, E., 36
Walsh, Rev., later Bishop, Robert, 68-9, 78, 79 et seq., 87
Walsh, Archbishop William, 113
Waterford city, 18, 21-2
Waters, C. M., 95
Weld, Bishop, 98
Wellesley, Capt. William, 111
Wellington, Duke of, 103, 106
West, John, 33
Weston, Br Michael Xavier, 149, 156
Whately, Archbishop Richard, 108, 109, 110, 112, 113
Whitty, Br Calasanctius, 154-5
Wilde, Oscar, 25
William of Orange, 5

Young, Arthur, 19, 22

Zino, Mons. John B., 100, 101